SOPHIE ROBERTSON has spent 18 years working in the recruitment industry in Australia, having been promoted from consultant to branch manager within 12 months, then running the most profitable of 30 branches for a national recruitment firm for five consecutive years.

As the director of Younique Coaching for the past seven years, Sophie has provided training and coaching services to recruiters and recruitment businesses, and is known for her passionate and motivating common-sense approach to recruitment challenges that gets results.

'I have worked in the world of industry and professional associations for over 20 years and there is one constant. Individuals with experience in their industry make the best facilitators and trainers. Industry continuous professional development prepared by respected, experienced industry professionals with an ability to communicate is highly sought after and valued. Sophie Robertson, FRCSA sits neatly into this area for the recruitment industry.

Sophie has been a highly valued and respected industry trainer for the RCSA for 6 years. Sophie consistently receives positive feedback on the training programs from a content and delivery viewpoint conducted on behalf of the RCSA.

Additionally Sophie truly values professionalism and best practice for this industry. I would recommend if you are looking for expertise in running a temp desk then look no further than this essential book and training by Sophie Robertson, FRCSA.'

— Steve Granland, RCSA CEO

For my sons Ruben and Fabian who are a constant source of inspiration, pride and joy.

SECRETS TO RUNNING A LUCRATIVE TEMP DESK

Captain Honey

www.captainhoney.com.au

First published in Australia in 2014 by Captain Honey Pty Ltd
PO Box 155, Byron Bay, NSW 2481, Australia

National Library of Australia Cataloguing-in-Publication Data

Robertson, Sophie.

Secrets to running a lucrative temp desk / Sophie Roberston
978-0-9874260-6-2 (pbk)
978-0-9874260-7-9 (epub)
978-0-9874260-8-6 (mobi)
978-0-9945552-0-5 (create space)
Temporary help services – Management
Employment agencies – Management

331.128068

Cover and internal design by Natalie Winter
Icons by Tasnadi Otto, Shutterstock

5 4 3 2 1   14 15 16 17 18

SECRETS TO RUNNING A LUCRATIVE TEMP DESK

SOPHIE ROBERTSON

CONTENTS

PART TWO

For managers and recruitment business owners

FOREWORD

In 2011 I was asked to describe what it takes to be a successful recruiter. It was such a simple question, but I had never really taken the time to sit and think through the best answer. I finally was able to answer the question, but it took twelve months and many hundreds of hours. I conducted twenty interviews with a variety of recruiters who had all succeeded in their careers. Some had floated large companies to earn their success, others ran businesses which were tiny in comparison but had remained consistently profitable through the decades, and had mastered the art of a work-life balance. What all had in common was that they had, in their own ways, forged brilliant careers in the tough and competitive but highly rewarding world of recruitment.

The book you are about to dive into is the accumulated knowledge of just such a brilliant career. Sophie has written a well-researched guide based on many years of personal experience and the results of exhaustive study into what makes a successful recruiter tick. It is full to the brim of useful instruction, insight and commentary on how you too can start and/or grow a successful on-hire temp and contract business. It's hard work, but the results for those who persevere are plentiful, the satisfaction unbeatable, and the achievement one to savour.

I wish you all the best with your journey to becoming a better person and a more successful recruiter, and hope you enjoy the rewards that come with it.

That journey begins now and with this book you'll be starting off with your best foot forward. Good luck.

Nicholas Beames
CEO, Astute Payroll
Author, *Different Thinking* (Astute Corporation, 2011)

INTRODUCTION

What is this book about and why am I writing it?

Put simply, this book is a 'how to' guide on running a best practice temp desk, which in turn means a profitable desk. It might even be the most profitable desk in your space, as mine was when I was at Ecco Personnel, now known as Adecco after its merger with Adia in 1996.

As to why I'm writing the book, after having worked in the recruitment industry for 18 years and having trained recruiters for the last seven years, it's a way of documenting and passing on what I consider to be best practice temp service.

One of my very first recruitment coaching clients, in 2007, asked if I could write a book that she could refer to when I wasn't with her. Back then I wasn't completely convinced that there was a market for such a book. But since that time I've coached numerous clients in how to set up a temp desk and I've run my temp desk master class workshop through the RCSA (Recruitment and Consulting Services Association) in Sydney, Melbourne, Perth, Brisbane and Auckland to sold out sessions, some not once or twice but three times over a 12-month period.

So there seems to not only be a need, but a hunger for information on how to do the temp/contracting consulting job well. In addition, it is and has always been my ambition to enhance the perception of our industry in the wider business community, and one way of doing this is to ensure that recruitment services are delivered exceptionally well, i.e. in an ethical and professional manner. In order to erase some people's perception that we are a low-barrier cowboy industry, we have to elevate our standards of operation, self-perception and professionalism. To do this, we need to deliver absolute best practice service, so we can be recognised as service professionals on a par with doctors and lawyers.

If you are reading this, then I am heartened by the fact that you want to improve your skill level to increase not only your own professionalism, but also the industry's overall. We can only expect and demand respect from the business community when we constantly strive to learn new skills and become adept at practising them. As Malcolm Gladwell (journalist and bestselling author who frequently uses research from social science, sociology, psychology and social psychology) points out in his bestselling book *Outliers* (Penguin, 2008), mastery comes through hard work and practice – 10,000 hours of practice to be precise. This is where I got my recruitment stripes; when I add up my hours of experience over 18 years of converting prospects to clients and identifying and managing temps, the total number of hours easily double the 10,000 and then some.

If you were in Australia in the early nineties, you may remember that it was the 'recession we had to have' according to the Honourable Paul Keating, our federal treasurer at the time. Can you imagine starting in recruitment when companies were literally laying people off by the hundreds? Well that's what it was like. When I phoned clients, they would ask: 'Why are you calling me, when I have to retrench 150 this week?' The number of people to be retrenched would vary, but otherwise the timbre of their responses was alarmingly similar.

Now when I look back, I am incredibly grateful that I'd picked tough economic times to start my recruitment career as I quickly learned what worked and what didn't. I learnt that three things rule in an economic downturn: persistence, relationship building and temps.

Persistence rules because we know statistically that people need to have on average four to seven contacts with us before they are ready to buy from us, unless it's a referred client.

Relationship building rules because unlike permanent recruitment, people have to trust you to provide the right skill set, before they give you a temp job order. Clients usually hire just one person to get a task done. For a permanent position, the client can interview several candidates and if the chosen candidate is lacking in certain skills, they can train them. For temps, they need to not just have the skill, but preferably excel at it as well. The temp's task is to get the job done expertly and then exit. That is unless they are offered a temp-to-permanent position with the company, which is great for you as you earn both temporary margins and a permanent placement fee. Plus it's a testament to your ability to find the right person with the right skill set and culture fit.

Temps rule because in uncertain economic times using temps is the perfect way for organisations to staff. They can use who they need, when they need and only pay for the hours they use. Also, when times are tough, clients downsize and consolidate permanent staffing numbers. Often they cut too close to the bone and leave their remaining employees to battle on with extra work. The inevitable results are burnt-out employees, more sick days and less productivity. This is the perfect time to introduce temps into a company where the client pays for what they use and can finish the temps up at any time. What I saw in these situations was that the temp solution gave clients peace of mind in the short term, and over time, the temps would quietly and organically integrate into the company. In short, the clients come to rely extensively on the temps' and your contribution to the running of the company.

On the back of a solid temp desk, I was able to run the most profitable branch out of 30 branches nationally at Ecco. A desk I had built up from scratch in a relatively new office in Parramatta, during an Australian recession that makes the Global Financial Crisis (GFC) of 2008 look like a small blip.

I eventually left Ecco after my maternity leave finished in 1997. When I returned to the workforce, I joined a small boutique agency, Integrity Personnel, which incorporated other brands: Accountancy Search, Retail Staffing Solutions plus a blue collar division. I remember at the interview I asked how many temps they had out and was told twelve (approximately 384 weekly hours) to which I said, 'That's not a temp desk! If you want a temp desk, I can help you build and grow one.'

So I did, and when I left after nine years of working on a part-time basis, the temp desk had on average 125 temps out, which equates to approximately 4000 hours per week. In the chapter about metrics, I'll discuss why temps need to be measured in hours as well as headcount to grow a temp desk. Many recruiters only talk about how many temps they have out, but this doesn't give an accurate enough picture of profit.

Okay, all that is history and what's it got to do with you? Well remember the GFC in 2008? Did you notice how many recruitment companies retrenched consultants? How our industry noticeably shrunk? But did you also notice how the companies with healthy temp desks not only survived, but actually thrived? Unless you were in a niche recruitment company and/or had a temp desk, the GFC almost certainly played havoc with your billings if you're a consultant, or your business if you're a recruitment business owner.

Here are ten solid reasons why you need to master running a temp desk:

1. It's recession and GFC proof; in fact challenging economic times are *boom* times for temps. While it's not too late to build a temp desk when times get tough, it's better to have the whole infrastructure set up and ready to roll. Otherwise the companies with established temp desks will steal the march on you as the clients already view them as trusted temporary staffing providers.

2. The temp recruitment industry is worth $19 billion annually in Australia (IBISWorld Key Industry Data 2013) and you want to ensure that you're getting a slice, or a bigger slice, of this considerable pie.

3. You never have to start the month with $0 on the board. If you only do permanent recruitment, you can have the best month ever, but when the calendar clicks to the first of the month, you're back to exactly zero dollars again, which can result in stress, and in worst case scenarios even burnout.

4. Each temp consultant can consistently bill approximately $56,000 per month without having to rely on perms. This is based on having 1000

hours per week at an average dollar margin of $13. If you think this is high and don't think you can charge it, you will change your mind if you ruthlessly implement the 'how-tos' shown in this book.

5. You will have better and more solid relationships with your clients. If your temps are part of the clients' key staff and you service the clients well, you will inevitably become a key factor in their business and success. Following my guide to best practice temp service means you will be speaking with your temp clients on a weekly basis.

6. Clients will be more loyal to you. Your job is to make the clients look good in their companies. When staffing is done well and engagement high, the clients get all the internal glory, which is how we want it!

7. You can become an industry expert very quickly and grow your desk almost without effort. Again I will show you how in this book.

8. As a dedicated temp consultant, you will be earning $134-$168,000 per annum (based on the industry average of a temp consultant expected to bill four to five times their own salary). These figures will naturally vary depending on the remuneration structure at your particular agency.

9. If you're a recruitment business owner, you add maximum value to your business by growing your temp desk, in case you ever want to sell up and ride off into the sunset. There is a bonus chapter on this exit strategy and how to get maximum multiples for your business written by merger and acquisition expert Rod Hore from HHMC (see chapter 18).

10. With more and more corporates hiring an increasing number of their permanent employees directly through their own talent acquisition teams, you are most likely losing perm revenue, so don't wait till it's too late. Lay the foundations for a solid temp desk and start earning part of the $19 billion dollars in revenue on offer right now!

This book is written for novice and experienced recruiters as well as for recruitment business owners. If you're a novice; good for you. You now get to learn the job as it should be done from the very start. No bad habits for you. If you're an experienced recruiter, then you might be reminded of a few things you'd forgotten and maybe even learn some new tips and tools. After all, if you've got nothing left to learn, you may as well roll over and give up. As Marshall Goldsmith (American leadership coach and author of management books) says: 'What got you here, won't get you there.'

If you're a recruitment business owner, you can use this book as a temp desk manual for training your staff and also as a GPS navigator for youself so you know what you need to keep an eye on.

While recruitment is not complicated, it is complex in that you need to understand what to do when and why.

Once you've read this book and followed my blueprint for the best temp desk on the planet, you will know when to do what, how to do it and what you need to do it. At the end of the book, I have provided a checklist of the things you need to do and think about to set up your best practice temp desk (see chapter 19).

Sound good? Well, let's get cracking!

When I use the word 'recruiter' in this book, I'm using it in the broadest sense to mean 'recruitment consultant' i.e., someone who attracts and enlists people and who gives advice on recruitment-related matters, which are very broad. For example your advice may pertain to behavioural descriptive interview questions, psychological tests, salary information, market intelligence, business wisdom and anything else relevant. In chapter 14, I discuss more in detail how you can become an expert and thus add value for your clients. Many people in the recruitment industry call themselves 'recruitment consultants' but do very little or no consulting at all. I believe that if you do not consult, that is share your recruitment-related expertise, then there is no value to the client in using you. They can train someone to shortlist resumes and interview; that is the bare bones of being a recruiter. This doesn't necessarily mean their internal recruiter can offer broad market salary advice, competitor and market intelligence, be up to date on the latest sourcing strategies, etc. This all belongs in the 'consulting' part, so in my view to be a good agency recruiter, you must recruit and consult to the client, and you must consult, advocate and work for your temps.

PART ONE

FOR CONSULTANTS WORKING A TEMP DESK

CHAPTER 1

THE MINDSET OF GREAT CONSULTANTS

Before I give you the complete toolkit on how to set up and run a profitable temp desk, you need you to examine your mindset. Everything starts and ends with the mind, so without the right mindset or understanding the three key success factors, the toolkit in itself will be useless. This way you get to determine whether you even want to embark on this temp journey with me or whether you're in the right career or hiring the right people to run your temp desk.

A consultant's mindset will determine the level of his or her success. As Stanford Professor of Psychology Carol Dweck (whose primary research areas deal with motivation, personality and development) outlines in her book *Mindset: The New Psychology of Success* (Ballantine Books, 2008), successful people have a 'growth mindset' as opposed to a 'fixed mindset'.

Fixed mindset people blame outer forces or circumstances for their lack of hours, sales or success. Have you heard recruiters blame the economy or maybe even on occasion done it yourself? Even if the 'pie' of available business has shrunk, you have to consider where the remaining business is and how you can acquire it. Growth mindset people ask questions as to how success can be achieved, rather than remain as passive victims of forces beyond their perceived control. A growth mindset means taking ownership of your skills and results, and realising that you can and must learn new and better skills. There is no pre-written script for how things turn out.

I have seen examples of recruiters unaccustomed to having to search for and win business due to the niche they've been in. Some recruiters have had the luxury of being able to cherry-pick their jobs, because they had no or very little competition. All I can say to them is 'Wow, you have been fortunate, but as things have now changed and the market has moved, what do you need to know and do, to not only survive but actually continue to thrive in your niche?' Upon reflection, I know how fortunate I was to start in the recruitment industry during the recession as I learnt to make cold calls, dig out where the business was and to convert prospects to clients. Apart from the growth mindset, we also need to incorporate the advice from Malcolm Gladwell's book about success that I mentioned in my introduction. In *Outliers*, Gladwell says there are two main factors to mastery of your craft, which is what success is: opportunity, i.e. the chance to practice your craft; and 10,000 hours of practice, a figure which emerged from all the case studies in his book.

Here are the three key factors that lead someone to success:

1. Having the right mindset
2. Opportunity to practice your craft
3. 10,000 hours of practice

As you are reading this book, you probably have a growth mindset already as you know you can improve your knowledge and skill level to set yourself up for success. If you are working as a recruiter, then every day is an opportunity for you. What's important here is that you choose to do the activities that matter. On any recruitment desk, we have an endless number of seemingly conflicting priorities: do you do reference checks, check your inbox, call clients, call temps, do the weekly report for your boss, etc.? Your choice will determine how much 'practice' you get at doing the activities that matter and therefore how good a temp consultant you become.

You must maintain focus and remember that great temp consultants do three critical tasks every day:

Finding quality temps: source, attract, secure and retain great temps with the desired skill sets.

Finding quality jobs for your temps: contacting clients by phone, in person or via email (the latter being the least effective way to find job orders and temp vacancies).

Matching the right temps to the right clients: regardless of whether that particular client has a job vacancy or not, if you know a particular client uses people with a particular hard-to-find skill, then call the client if you have someone available and ask if they have that need now. Boral used to need cost accountants and as they were rare, I'd always keep an eye out for them. Liquorland used to need accountants with Excel Vlookup skills; again I was always on the lookout and would ask every accountant I interviewed to see how confident they were in this particular skill. When I found one, I'd phone the client immediately. If you know it's a needle-in-a-haystack skill, then don't wait till the client phones you and then start looking. Your chances of getting those hours become very low percentage. Good temp consultants are proactive, not reactive.

During my recruitment career I've seen many good people leave this industry and it's never been due to the fact that they didn't know how to interview or recruit. It's always due to their lack of skills on the sales side. Some believed that they weren't cut out to do sales; this is what Professor Dweck would refer to as having a fixed mindset, as we can always improve our skills and capabilities, if we want to. Others have not known how to overcome their own aversion to selling and their self-image as a salesperson.

The good news about having a fixed mindset is that you can decide to change it to a growth mindset any time you want to, by taking responsibility for your results and asking questions around how you can convert more sales.

Regarding aversion to sales, you need to first be crystal clear that recruitment is a sales job. Think about it: you sell the job, the opportunity, the company to the temp. You sell the temp to the company. By selling, I mean pointing out and emphasising the 'benefits' of 'what's in it for me' ('WIIFM') i.e. why it's good for them to do this assignment or why this temp is right for this client. I don't mean manipulating the client or temp to do something they don't want to do or something that may be detrimental to them. The latter is how many people unconsciously think of sales and sales people. Yet when the discussion is lifted to the conscious level, most people can cite examples of how impressed they have been with a knowledgeable and caring salesperson who helped them out. You need to focus on defining what good sales service is and identifying with that type of salesperson, rather than the manipulative, sleazy one you may have in your mind and therefore are distancing yourself from.

There's a saying that the most important sale you will ever make is to yourself. This is completely true, as how you view yourself will inform your behaviour, which will ultimately determine your results and success. You need to come to terms with the fact that recruitment is a 'sales' job, that a recruiter is a 'sales' person, and believe that you are providing real value to your clients. To not make contact with a prospect is potentially depriving someone of benefitting from your expertise. This is how I viewed it when I phoned a prospect; if I didn't phone them, they could be getting second-class service and not even know it. They should at least have the opportunity to say no to what I had to offer.

Once you are okay with being in a sales environment, then read on. Even if you are a resourcer and don't have business development responsibilities, your job is to make the jobs or your company sound attractive to your candidates and temps, which meets my definition of selling.

CHAPTER 2

WHAT IS A TEMP DESK?

In Australia the recruitment industry is worth $22 billion dollars per annum with 86% of this income coming from temps and contractors. The rest comes from permanent recruitment fees.

The majority of recruitment companies traditionally have a perm desk where permanent recruitment is done for and on behalf of a client.

Some of these companies will also have a temp desk, where a group of skilled temporaries and contractors are available for work and managed by one or more consultants.

Permanent recruiters need to understand what the client needs a potential employee to do and who will be the best fit from a cultural and succession-planning point of view. The recruiter then makes a 'match' and gets paid a once-off fee for finding the best available person.

Temporary recruiters have to do the same plus be able to make multiple matches for each new temp assignment plus manage a remote workforce plus ensure that temps and clients are kept constantly happy by providing superior ongoing service.

For perm recruiters the service ends once the person is placed (apart from the guarantee checks). For temp recruiters, the service begins in earnest when the temp is placed.

Recruitment companies have different models of running temp desks; some have a combined or mixed desk, which means the recruiter does both permanent and temporary recruitment for their clients and others will be dedicated temp consultants who don't do permanent recruitment. My belief is that to have a successful, growing and profitable temp desk, you need to have specialist temp consultants for three reasons:

1. They are actually two quite different jobs. While they both recruit, their focus is on different things. Perm recruiters can look more in depth at a person's long-term career goals. Their placement timeline can be quite long as some companies have long, protracted hiring processes, so they need to be patient and content to work at that speed. While perm recruiters can make recommendations to their clients on which candidate to hire, they don't have the deciding vote. Temp recruiters will thrive on speed and having the adrenalin pumping when put under pressure, e.g. when a client calls and need eight data entry operators and they have 20 minutes to fill them. Temp recruiters have to be excellent people managers as they manage their temp workforce remotely. They have the final say in who does which assignment, so they need to be able to take full responsibility for their choice and stand by it, if challenged by the client.

2. If recruiters run a combined desk, they will often be conflicted about what to do. There may be a client who needs second interviews organised for a permanent position where the placement fee is $12,000, and also a temp job available for a week which is going to net them $500 in temp margin. Many recruiters will choose to do the perm work first, which may mean that they lose the temp job, so that client isn't being serviced and also a temp misses out on the work. It's a conflict that a consultant doesn't need to be subject to.

3. Due to having to change speed and focus, a combined desk is always detrimental to growing temp hours, which is detrimental to the agency's income. Temp income is like having money in the bank as long-term assignments just tick over all the time and provide cash flow, certainty and solid profits.

Temps are often referred to as the 'bread and butter' of an agency while the perms are the 'cream'. Or the temp income is what keeps the lights on, as it's income that can be relied upon. You can get a better understanding of why this is when you read Chapter 18, which focuses on valuation of a recruitment business for sale.

While a temp is working, the consultant earns a margin for every hour they work and sometimes even a margin for when they don't work e.g. public holiday payments, if applicable. If the temp is exceptional (which they will be once you implement the processes in this book) you will often earn a temp-to-permanent placement fee as well. This is when the client offers the temp a permanent position with their company and it's accepted by the temp. Or, you get to place that temp with another client and the whole business of earning starts again! Does it get any better?

Temps are usually called in to perform a specific task or to cover a specific position, so it's important to know exactly what they will be doing. The more information you can glean from the outset, the better equipped you will be to make the match. It's not enough to know the client needs a receptionist for the day. You need to know what type of switchboard they use, how many incoming/outgoing lines does it have, do calls need to be announced when they are put through, will there be paging over an intercom system. Also you need to find out if other duties are required, such as typing, organising lunches, boardroom, preparing the mail, or doing big mail-outs.

For purposes of simplicity, in this book, I will refer to temps, casuals, on-hire staff and contractors as 'temps'. Please refer to the glossary at the back of this book for definitions of these and other relevant terms.

Note that clients often use the terms temps, casuals and contractors interchangeably, so it's your job as a consultant to assist the clients to define and specify what they mean and what they want. This is your area of expertise, so share it.

A 'genuine' temp desk will have temps with documented skills ready to go when and where needed. It is not a genuine, professional temp desk when your client asks you for a temp and you scrounge around trying to find someone to see if they are interested in going to that assignment. Sure if your temp desk is busy, fast moving and growing, there may be a certain degree of scrounging, but that will be due to your increasing temp job orders, not due to you not having temps set up and ready to go out to work at a moment's notice.

Skilled temps almost need to be thought of as an off-the-shelf 'product' that you can access any time. To do this you need to be proactive and constantly recruit for temps. You need to know what type of temps your clients need and the type of temps you want to specialise in.

CHAPTER 3

WHEN DO CLIENTS NEED TEMPS?

When I first started in recruitment, I used to phone clients and ask if they needed a temp, which was a hugely ineffective way of servicing clients and growing my desk. As a recruiter, you are the expert in problem solving and therefore you need to know when the clients can use a temp to alleviate a problem. So here are some examples of situations where a temp can cover for clients:

- holidays
- sick leave
- maternity leave
- long service leave
- carer's leave
- bereavement leave
- seasonal peaks, e.g. Christmas
- industry peaks, e.g. September for the electronics industry
- gaps created by redundancies

- end of financial year, which can be March, June, September or December depending on where the client company is from and where they report to in the world
- while recruiting for permanent positions to allow enough time to find the right person
- WorkCover return-to-work situations where the returning worker may be on reduced duties or time
- training, i.e. when everyone is at training and someone is needed to man the office
- external temp trainers used to up-skill internal staff
- company events, e.g. Melbourne Cup lunch, Christmas lunch where all staff are attending
- product launches
- trade exhibitions and fairs
- moving offices
- implementing new systems, e.g. new computer systems
- permanent headcount hiring freeze, where they can only hire temps as they aren't part of 'headcount'
- secondment of staff to other areas of the business
- special projects, e.g. working on tenders, implementing LEAN efficiency processes

This list is just to get you started and is by no means exhaustive. The great thing about building a temp desk is that you are only limited by your imagination. Don't be limited by your clients' imagination.

With the examples above, you can now have meaningful conversations with your client about what's going on in their company rather than just asking if they need a temp. Once you know what's going on, you can use your expertise to suggest a temp as a solution for their specific situation.

Think about your job as solving a problem rather than providing a temp.

The latter breeds an attitude of providing a 'bum on seat', which cheapens what we do and hugely restricts our earning potential and the opportunity to truly provide value to our clients.

CHAPTER 4

HOW TO SET UP A TEMP DESK

To illustrate the process, let's say we're starting up a white-collar temp desk. These are the steps you need to follow.

1. Determine the categories of temps that you will be supplying

For our white-collar example:

- filing clerks
- receptionists
- PAs (personal assistants) and EAs (executive assistants)
- data entry operators
- call centre operators
- customer service clerks
- accounts payable clerks
- accounts receivable clerks
- collections officers

- payroll clerks
- accountants – financial, management, cost
- financial controllers

2. Determine the skills needed for each category

This will help you to take the right details for a temporary job order and help you to know what to ask when interviewing temps. Your job as a temp consultant is to ensure that your temps can confidently do the assignments you send them to. The temps have to feel comfortable and the clients need to receive value for money. Skills and experience needed in our scenario include:

Filing clerks: alphabetical filing (must be good spellers), numerical filing. A temp with dyslexia may find filing difficult.

Receptionists: type of switchboards used, number of lines and extensions, number of calls received per hour, number of visitors received per day, intercom usage for paging, typing and word-processing skills, vocabulary and voice, personal presentation.

PAs and EAs: Word, Excel, PowerPoint skills, diarising, event organisation, screening phone calls, minute taking, shorthand, personal shopping.

Data entry operators: fast and accurate alphabetical, numerical or alphanumerical data entry.

Call centre operators: inbound, outbound, order taking, returns, complaints, help desk, volume of incoming/outgoing calls, escalation process.

Customer service operators: as for call centre operators.

Accounts payable clerks: manual, system/packages, number of invoices, payment cycle, matching and batching, EFT (electronic funds transfer), cheque runs.

Accounts receivable clerks: system/packages, number of debtors, amounts, days outstanding, invoicing.

Collections officers: working off print out or computer, number of debtors, amounts chased, days outstanding, number of phone calls per day.

Payroll officers: frequency of payroll, number of pays, awards, enterprise agreements, payroll system.

Accountants: financial, management, cost, system/packages, reporting, other duties e.g. staff supervision or reports

Financial controllers: system/packages, staff reports, reporting deadlines.

3. Determine how you will test their skills

Some examples of tests might be:

- spelling tests
- basic numerical/mathematical tests
- typing tests
- data entry tests; numerical and alphanumerical
- Word, Excel, PowerPoint tests
- shorthand tests

Determine whether you want to test their skills in your office or whether you are happy for them to log in online and do the test from home. The danger of them doing it from a place of their choice is that theoretically, they could get someone else to do the test for them and you won't know until you send them to a job and the client tells you the temp doesn't have the skills required. Also if allowed to do the test in their own time, they may not get around to it, which means you won't be able to use them. My recommendation is for them to do the testing while they are in your office for the interview, then they are ready to go to any assignment and you have peace of mind knowing that they *can* do what you told the client they could do. It's critical that you know what the temp can do, as temps are needed to fill a particular gap with very specific skills.

There are various companies who offer skill testing software, Qwiz is one example.

4. Specify your benchmarks

These are the minimum standards that you will accept for a temp (determined by the test results):

- spelling: 98% accuracy
- maths: 95% accuracy
- typing: min 55 wpm with 98% accuracy
- data entry: alpha 8000 keystrokes per hour, numerical 10,000 keystrokes with 98% accuracy (some clients may say that speed is not important as long as the temp is accurate, but as a professional temp consultant, your job is to provide temps with both speed and accuracy)
- Word, Excel, PowerPoint: basic, intermediate, advanced (it's helpful here to have a copy of their test results, so you know what they can do, e.g. they may be 'advanced' in Excel, but never had to do Vlookup)
- shorthand: minimum 100 wpm, 120 wpm is preferable

Benchmarks are very important as these can be used to compare skills of temps. If a client asks you why your temps cost $3 more per hour than another consultant's, you can ask what sort of skills the cheaper temps have. More often than not, your competitor will not have advised the client or they may not even know themselves!

With clients, it's important that you do not get sucked into a discussion about price (the actual dollars and cents), but keep the discussion about value. Value which you can demonstrate by showing that a faster and more accurate data entry operator will get the job done quicker without the need for someone else to correct their work, which is in fact cheaper in the long run. The cheaper temp may require more hours to do the same job and require someone to both check and correct their work. Always discuss value to ensure that the client is aware that when comparing temps, they must ensure they are not only comparing apples with apples, but that they are actually comparing Red Delicious with Red Delicious. Otherwise it would be like going to a Mercedes Benz dealer and asking why their cars can't be had for the price of a Toyota. Here the point about value versus price is very stark and obvious. So it is with temps; remember that if the client wants to compare, you need to demonstrate your expertise by explaining the value gained by having higher skilled and more accurate temps. That it would be completely fallacious to compare two people's skill levels without truly understanding what they are capable of.

5. Recruit three to five temps in each category

That's three to five available people with the benchmarked skills for each job, e.g. five clerks, five receptionists, five accountants. Remember that some people can belong in several categories; if you have a PA, the chances that she can answer a switchboard are quite high. The chances that she wants to do it are on the other hand not as high, while some will downright refuse to do it, which segues nicely into our next chapter on how to interview for temps.

6. Have a standard response time

Best practice temp desks offer immediate service; I've always worked on a 20-minute call back service where the client would have their booking confirmed within 20 minutes of calling a job order in. Or if I couldn't give them a confirmed name in that time, I'd still call them back within 20 minutes to let them know when I could fill the job by. Or, if I wasn't confident that I could fill the job, I'd ask them to go to another agency. The lead time till the job starts may simply be too short. Never take up all the available time trying to fill a job if you are unsure whether you can, as you've effectively made it impossible for any other agency to fill the job as well, which means you've left the client in the lurch. This is cardinal sin!

Although we focussed in this example on starting up a white-collar temp desk, the above process can be used to set up any type of temp desk: blue-collar, professional, retail, medical, hospitality, home care, etc. Same process, different categories and skill sets. If blue-collar, retail or hospitality you will need more people available in each category as these are traditionally high volume temp desks. The number of available temps you require in each category will be governed by your clients' needs. The suggested three to five is to get a temp desk started from scratch, so you have some temps to market out and fill jobs with.

Remember that what you're selling when you sell temps is peace of mind. This means that your client does not have to fret about whether you're going to fill the job or when you might call back, which allows them to get on with their own job. The main advantage to you of filling your jobs in 20 minutes is that the client knows you're going to have the job booked, so they don't give the job out to other agencies. By acting effectively and efficiently, you fill more jobs, have more temps out working and bill more hours! The client is happy as they know you've taken care of the job; they can relax. The temp is happy as they know they have a job to go to. You and your boss are happy as you're growing your hours, desk and income.

CHAPTER 5

HOW TO RECRUIT AND MANAGE GREAT TEMPS

As we've seen, recruiting for temps is vastly different to recruiting for perms. For example for perms you want to know what the candidate's long-term career goals and aspirations are. For temps this is not really necessary information and can even distract you.

Essentially there are two types of temps:

People who really want a permanent job, but are willing to temp in the meantime.

People who choose to temp for their own reasons, e.g. they might be studying, travelling, only need to work part time, want flexibility, don't like to work in the same place day in, day out, have religious reasons, want school holidays off, are writing a book, or any number of other reasons. Sometimes these temps are referred to as professional temps.

It's important to know and understand each person's motivation for temp work, so you can do the best for them and your client. If a client wants a long-term temp (six months plus) it's better to place someone who actually will be happy with this assignment rather than someone who really wants the security of a permanent job. Because if and when that candidate gets a permanent job offer, they will most likely leave your temp job and leave you and your client in the lurch. It's up to you to prevent this from happening and to control as many variables as you can. In temp recruitment if you can do the job properly the first time, it will save you lots of re-filling and problem solving later on.

You want to be the temp consultant who can anticipate problems and practise proactive prevention as this is a sure-fire way to win! Understanding human nature and using empathy are vital traits of a top temp consultant. If you're concerned something might go wrong it most likely will, unless you take precautions.

Here's an example. Your temp normally works for $33 per hour and you ask them to do a long-term assignment at $29.50 per hour. If they pull out on you for a better paying job, this is something you could have and should have anticipated. Rather than complain about the temp's loyalty, examine your own. If you truly understand their motivation for temping and what will keep them happy, then work in their interest and they will repay you with loyalty, commitment and referrals.

If possible, aim to have at least 50% of your temp pool from the people who choose to temp. It will make your life a lot easier. That's not to say that you don't want to have any permanent candidates in your temp pool, but the turnover rate is high, which makes it harder to grow your hours by adding more temps and also your service to your clients will suffer as you can't offer the same temps back to them.

WHERE YOUR TEMPS COME FROM

- Permanent candidates, who may wish to temp either until they find a perm job or instead of one. Some candidates are happy to work as a temp or contractor if they are kept in work. Challenges tend to arise if they are seeking a bank loan as banks don't consider temporary work to be as secure as a permanent job. This is interesting as there is a global trend towards 'casualisation' of the workforce.

- Advertising: online platforms such as Seek, your agency website, university intranets, print media (although minimal now), trade publications.
- Word of mouth: if you already have some temps out and you provide proper temp care, people temping for other agencies will seek you out for different reasons: more work available, better work with better companies, better pay rates, better temp benefits, better service. These are all factors that contribute to a temp deciding whom they want to represent them and whom they prefer to work for.
- Talking to people when you're out socially and asking them what they do. Always carry business cards!
- Referrals from clients, temps and perm candidates. You need to have a formal referral incentive program, although providing good service is usually the *best* incentive for people to refer you to other temps.
- Headhunting: if you have heard about a particularly good temp, you can ask if they are happy with their current agency. Temps are like perm candidates; they can choose who they want to work for and when. Just like any employer, if a temp agency doesn't look after their temps, then they will move.
- Social media: LinkedIn, Facebook, Twitter etc.
- Trade fairs: exhibitions for specific trades or groups, e.g. for the electronics industry, Australian Defence Force, university students.
- Booths in shopping centres: e.g. I set up a booth in a Westfield shopping centre at lunchtime and handed out flyers and encouraged people to register if they were looking to change their jobs or they were unemployed. Once I even convinced a store manager to change industries and switch to working in recruitment at one of these booths.
- Agency open days where people can register.
- Networking events: most industries have their own events, e.g. the credit industry gathers at Australian Institute of Credit Management events;

doctors go to professional development conferences. Find out where the people you want to attract go, and make sure you're there too.

SERVICE MATTERS

CASE STUDY: *Boral Masonry*

Once when we were at Boral seeing our temps, I was approached by a woman who worked in their accounts department. I had seen her before on previous visits and assumed she was a permanent employee. On this occasion she asked if she could transfer to our agency. Her reasoning was that she had temped there for several years and she had *never* had her agency or consultant contact her during that time for anything other than to chase her time sheet. Through seeing and hearing us call and visit our temps regularly, she saw that she could be part of a team if she worked through us, rather than be the temp whom her agency forgot!

This was frankly appalling, but not at all uncommon. I explained to her that she would first have to contact her agency to resign and ask Boral whether they were okay with her transferring to our payroll. Then and only then would I take her on. Understand that this is very different to a situation where I approached her and asked her whether she wanted to transfer to our payroll for the same client. That would be considered 'poaching', which is unethical.

On the other hand we have to accept that temps are free agents just like you, and can choose to work for whomever they choose, which is what happened in this case.

We got hours just by displaying our temp care, expertise and professionalism! Temps are real people, who like to know they are valued and not taken for granted. Some recruiters adopt a 'place and forget' attitude to temps. This is a very slippery slope that will increase your vulnerability, as clients may hire your temps directly without paying you a temp-to-perm fee. When you look after your temps and care about them, they will be on your side and look after your interests and your livelihood. The clincher in the Boral story was that when the temp resigned from the other agency and told them why, they did not have anything to say!

I can only hope for their sake and their temps' sake, that they have since improved their service.

As a postscript, clients will normally take the side of the temp who wants to transfer, as they value the temp and want to keep them. The client at Boral fully supported the temp's wishes and informed the agency that they wanted to employ the temp through us, as it was the temp's choice in the end.

Poaching temps is against the RCSA's Code of Ethics. The RCSA (Recruitment and Consulting Services Association) is the recruitment industry's ethical, educational and governing body in Australia and New Zealand. Unfortunately recruitment is still a self-regulated industry in Australia, which means membership is not compulsory. As such the RCSA does not have any power over non-members which is why the entry bar to the recruitment industry is very low and why there are some unethical agencies who give the whole industry a bad name.

I believe you need to display your expertise and professionalism at every opportunity as you are in a service business, which is vastly different to selling a physical product. Your reputation is invaluable: guard it, enhance it and build on it.

The point of the Boral example is that the temp could clearly see that she was not valued by her employer and that our temps were. Some agencies try to have their temps sign an 'exclusive' agreement, where they agree not to work for anyone else. This is, in my opinion, not worth the paper it's written on. Even married people get divorced. So why can't temps leave their agency, if they're not happy? How would you feel, if you couldn't leave your employer if you were unhappy?

Treat your temps well; value and appreciate them, as they are your employees. The fact that they turn up every day to your client's business makes them your best or worst ambassadors. It's up to you to look after them. If you don't know how; think about what you want from your boss. After having asked this question in many workshops, I know the answers are:

- recognition
- feeling valued

- appreciation
- being rewarded
- being part of the team
- being in the loop

What are you doing to deliver the above benefits to your temps?

Summary

- Treat your temps with the same dignity and respect with which you would like to be treated.
- Temp loyalty is cultivated by showing you care about them and their individual preferences.
- Always be ethical; if a temp wants to transfer onto your payroll, ensure it's done correctly, so there can be no doubt that you didn't instigate the transfer.

CHAPTER 6

THE ESSENCE OF THE TEMP INTERVIEW

We talked about treating your temps well, so you can retain their services for you and your clients. But how do you identify and recruit the good – and great – temps?

WHAT, WHEN AND HOW FAR?

There are three critical questions to ask when you interview temps:

What *will* you do? Notice this is different to 'what can you do?' Just because they can answer a switchboard, doesn't mean they want to in a temp assignment. Remember your job is to keep them happy, so they will be good ambassadors for you and keep your clients happy.

When can you start, and for how long? This means exactly when, so not 'asap' but 'tomorrow morning and I'm happy to commit to a maximum of three months at a time'.

How far will you go? This relates to travel and again it needs to be very specific, so not 'half an hour's drive' as that can mean different distances depending on where they drive from and the time they start their journey. I discuss and get commitment on specific suburbs and locations they will go to.

As I have 20 minutes to fill a job, I don't have time to ask them if they will go to a location, do the type of work required or whether they will commit to the timeframe. I need to know their answers to all those questions when I pick up the phone to book them in.

I tend to 'tell' them rather than ask. So it sounds like this: 'Hi Susie, I've got a great job for you starting tomorrow for two weeks doing exactly what you've been used to and it's only 30 minutes from home.' Then I give them the details and confirm them. It's an assumptive approach but you can use it, if you've done the work of asking the 'what', 'where' and 'how long' questions at the interview. I don't say: 'I'm calling to see if you're interested in doing this job'. There is simply no reason for them not to do it, unless they aren't committed.

Sometimes you can't quite match all of someone's criteria. Then you can say something like: 'I know you said you didn't want to work in the city, but it's only for two days and if you do this for me, you will be first cab off the rank for any jobs close to your home. I need to call in a favour.' Most temps will do the odd assignment if you acknowledge it isn't their preferred job (so they know you listened and care) and you have a good relationship with them. If you can't get your temps to do your assignments, you're either not being firm enough or they don't respect you.

DEFINE THE TEMP'S SKILLS

Further to the 'what will you do' question, you need to determine (and then test) the skills that they are prepared to use on a temp assignment.

Have a tick sheet with very specific skills that they can select, e.g. Ericsson switchboard, rather than just switchboard, and alphabetical or numerical filing, rather than just filing. Just because they've used one switchboard doesn't mean they won't need training to use another. It's vital for you to be able to tell your clients exactly the skills the temp has and what training they will need, if any.

Having happy clients is partly about managing expectations. For example, if you tell a client that your temp has previously used an Ericsson switchboard with 10 incoming lines and 200 extensions for 12 months, they will expect them to be proficient with it, whereas their expectations will be very different if the temp only did relief reception work one day a week.

You need to know specifically what the temp can do so that you can pass that knowledge on to your client. Likewise you need to know specifically what the client wants the temp to do in the assignment, so the temp knows what to expect. This is the area of expertise that defines your competence as a temp consultant, i.e. the ability to take a thorough and accurate job order and to find the closest match in skills that you can. If you are not really specific about the information required, the probability of getting it wrong is high, with the end result that you lose credibility and trust with both client and temp.

You also need to ensure that the temp has a valid working visa if they are not a citizen or permanent resident. For some niches like blue-collar manufacturing clients, they may also need relevant tickets to perform the work, e.g. a forklift licence.

SPECIFICITY IS GOLD

I am obsessed with some things, and one of them I express by saying: '*specificity is gold*'. Anyone who has been coached, trained or mentored by me knows that this is one of my deep beliefs.

Cast your mind back to a situation of conflict with either a client or temp. Or even in a personal relationship. Consider whether the conflict arose because someone wasn't specific enough? Usually this is the case.

It may have been you *assuming* the client had read and agreed to your Terms of Business, but as you neglected to talk to them and to get their express agreement *and* signature, there may now be a conflict *after* you found them the temp. Or worse, after the temp has already done the job and needs to be paid!

Or it may be that you asked the temp to call you if they couldn't go to an assignment, but you didn't specify *when* they had to call you, so they called your client in the morning and only phoned you in the afternoon after missing a whole day of work!

There are countless examples, but I'm sure you have some of your own. The way to master the temp consulting job is to reflect when something goes wrong: 'what could I be more specific about to avoid a similar situation next time?'

By being really *specific*, you get rid of assumptions and have a real chance of preventing a problem before it even arises. Look at your potential conflict situations and prevent them from recurring by instilling some 'rules'.

RULES MATTER

Have you ever played poker or Monopoly with others and at some point into the game experienced disagreements? People saying, 'that's not how we play it,' or similar? Well, this can easily be avoided, if you set out the rules from the beginning and get agreement from all participants. It's exactly the same with temp, candidate and client relationships. Being in control is part of displaying your expertise and professionalism. If you know what to do, but skip the steps, quite frankly you deserve the problems you encounter later on.

So the next step of the interview is to explain how you need to work with your temps in order to deliver as many assignments as possible for them, and to gain their agreement to your 'rules'. In my experience in sales and in life, people will agree to do what you ask if you tell them what benefits they will get out of it. In other words: what's in it for them.

This is how I do it and what I say:

'We work on a 20-minute call back service, which means that we call our clients back within 20 minutes of them giving us a job and we give them the name of the temp booked for the assignment regardless of whether the job is to start tomorrow or in three week's time. What I need to know from you is whether I can book you in without speaking to you in case I can't get hold of you? I know what you will do and where you'll go so all I need is your availability. You need to tell me if your availability changes as 20 minutes go very quickly and I simply can't be on the phone asking if you're available to do that assignment. Imagine if I had to call five temps to ask if they are available. I'd use up all my time and not be able to give the clients top-level service. The happier our clients are, the more jobs we have, which means that I can keep you in work. It's okay if your availability changes, but you must let me know immediately and *not* when I have a job for you. If I know you're not available, I just won't call you. Better for both of us.'

I then go on to explain: 'It's helpful if you haven't heard from me and I know you're available, for you to call or text me around 3pm to see if there are any jobs for the following day. This also keeps you at the forefront of everyone's minds and we know you're keen to work with us. Does this sound okay? Let's start today so you can get into the habit.'

This part of the interview process is *critical* and must not be skipped or glossed over as doing this well will save you time and effort at a later date. It's about temp control and setting the parameters of the relationship. If you don't tell them the 'rules', they will make up their own. It's a great litmus test to see if they call you the first day you ask them to. If they do, they have every potential to become a great temp. If they don't, this should act as a warning bell; explain the process to them again, get their commitment again and test them again.

Another rule to set applies to when they are actually on assignment. Tell them that you want to ensure their happiness in a job and therefore would like to speak to them on a weekly basis. Jobs change and sometimes they may get asked to perform additional duties, which may warrant a pay rise. Or sometimes the workload may increase and they may want to avail themselves of the overtime option, which you can help facilitate for them. Tell them it's best if they call you when they have a spare couple of minutes as you may call them at a busy time. Again get agreement from them that they will do this. Remember the Boral example? The other agency had completely lost touch with their temp and were just slowly raking in the margin she was earning for them week in, week out – until they lost her.

Your agency may also have rules around mobile phone, Facebook and internet usage while at work, for instance only using them for work purposes or during the lunch break.

Now you need to tell the temp about how you pay and what they need to do to get paid. I would advise that you use the same words at every temp interview, so you know you've said it and you have a consistent interview process.

If your week goes from Monday to Friday, you might want them to email you their time sheet by 5pm on Fridays. Advise them on when their pay will be in their account. Depending on which award you pay them under, pay day might be the following Tuesday. It's their responsibility to give you their correct bank details and also to give you their tax file number, so they can be taxed appropriately. Tell them to call you if their manager isn't around to verify their hours, so you can chase up a signature for them. It's very important that you pay the temps on time (to keep them happy) but also so you can invoice your client as well. You can't count the hours as billed if you don't invoice!

TEMP AVAILABILITY LIST

Once the temp has left the interview, you must put all the information you have gathered on an availability list. How good this list is will to a large extent determine how quickly you can grow your hours, because as we've seen, a comprehensive and specific list means that the temps will actually do the assignments when you contact them.

The availability list needs to have on it the following information:

Name: The name that they prefer to be called (for example, Sandra Citizen may rather be called Sandie).

Phone number: Their number and an alternative such as their wife's or dad's.

Location: Where they live, so you can assess travel time. Also include where they will travel to.

Skills: Details of their experience and the standards they have achieved in your tests.

Transport: Do they have their own car or do they need to work close to public transport?

Start date: If they say they are available asap, ask if that means tomorrow.

Sometimes they'll say 'Oh no, not that soon,' so be specific and nail it down to a date.

How long they are available: The maximum length assignment they are willing to take.

I cannot stress enough how important this list and the integrity of the information on it is. Without this, it's impossible for you to fill a job quickly and efficiently. If you offer a 24-hour service, you need to have this list with you all the time, whether in hard copy or in easily searchable electronic format.

VERBAL REFERENCE CHECKS

Finally, you must do verbal reference checks with a prospective temp's referees. In my career, I have seen some fraudulent written references that were only unearthed when we phoned to do the verbal reference checks. One referee said they had never given that person the written reference that we had a copy of! It turned out the applicant had stolen the company's letterhead before leaving and was forging the manager's signature.

Through verbal reference checks you can confirm specific details about someone's flexibility and common sense, which are critical traits in a good temp. Here are some questions that you need to ask in a verbal reference check:

- Did Joe show common sense? Can you give me an example of when Joe demonstrated common sense in his job?
- Would you describe Joe as a flexible employee? Can you give an example of this flexibility?
- How does Joe perform when thrown into a new environment/team? What type of new situation has he been thrust into while working for you?
- Was Joe reliable and punctual?
- Would you recommend Joe to a future employer?
- Would you rehire Joe?

- Are you the person who hires temporary staff for your company?
- (If the answer to the above question is yes) As Joe is available for work right now, what do you have that I can book him for?

Ask the potential temp about the referees they have put down. You will need at least two referees whom you can call and they need to be people the temp reported to, preferably in temp jobs and/or their most recent jobs. If the former, this will also immediately provide you with potential sales leads as you know the referees use temps. Take the opportunity to ask who hires temps in their company and offer the temp that you're reference checking straight back to them. Quickest and easiest temp jobs you're ever going to uncover.

WALKING DOLLAR TEMPS

If you've been in recruitment before, you will recognise a 'walking dollar temp' when you see one. They are the ones you can send anywhere and they will impress your clients. Temps are not like a shelf product that you can store until you sell them. If you don't keep your temps in work, they will work elsewhere and you've lost them. This is true for any good temp, but for a walking dollar temp, their shelf life is almost non-existent. I would market these temps straight away, preferably while they are still in my office. How impressed would they be if you got them a job before they left the interview? Call 10 of your clients and market that temp to them. In my experience, when I did this, I would get at least two jobs within 24 hours. You can also ask your temp to nominate five to 10 companies they would love to work for. Call them while the temp is in front of you. The loyalty you get from them by displaying that you're actually working proactively to get them a job cannot be underestimated. Even if you don't manage to secure them an assignment before they leave your office, they will work within with your rules as they can see you're genuinely trying to secure them a job.

If you can't get them a job before they leave your office, promise them that you will pull out all stops to place them. You can ask them in return not to take another assignment as you will be marketing them heavily. To be fair to them, give them a deadline, e.g. 36 or 48 hours, which will also provide you with the urgency to hunt out that job order for them. Your pay-off will be the strong likelihood of the assignment being extended or even going perm as your client will also recognise the quality of the temp.

Characteristics of a walking dollar temp

- well groomed
- excellent skills
- friendly
- adaptable
- flexible
- reliable
- intelligent
- common sense in spades

CHAPTER 7

HOW TO SELL TEMPS

Now you've got all those short-shelf-life temps on your books you must get some job orders, or you'll lose the temps, and then when you do get job orders, you won't be able to provide a quick and efficient temp service.

A recruitment consultant is like a juggler who is constantly juggling three balls: these are the three critical tasks of a successful consultant that I've mentioned before.The three balls are:

Finding quality temps: source, attract, secure and retain great temps with the desired skill sets.

Finding quality jobs for your temps: contacting clients by phone, in person or via email.

Matching the right temps to the right clients: regardless of whether that particular client has a job vacancy or not, offering the client someone who you know would suit their business especially if their skill set is hard to find.

Just like a juggler, *all* three balls must be in the air at once. If you only concentrate on getting more temps without calling clients to find jobs, you will lose the majority of them as their shelf life is extremely short. Most temps can't afford to sit around and wait for you to find them jobs. If on the other hand you only do business development without replenishing your temp pool, you won't have any temps to fill the jobs when you get them. Therefore you need to dedicate time to all of the three critical tasks.

The very best recruiters do these three tasks *every* day. They don't get sidetracked with other things. And let's face it, there really are a lot of tasks on a temp desk that are peripheral to the main game: answering emails, returning phone calls, doing reference checks. While these tasks are necessary, they are not critical. By critical, I mean you will either fail at being a good temp consultant *or* you will have huge peaks and troughs in your hours and billings. These peaks and troughs are commonly referred to in the industry as champagne and razor blades. Champagne when you have a great month and razor blades for when you have nothing on the board and nothing in the pipeline. This is obviously *not* the best way of building your career or income stream. Also, some recruitment companies are not willing to 'carry' you, if you have too many razor-blade months. So for your own peace of mind, earning capacity, reputation, professional growth and work security, make sure you do your three critical tasks *every* day. Yes there will be days where you might be putting out fires and you don't have a whole lot of time to make those calls, but even if you only manage four sales calls, that's better than none. It's a matter of establishing a habit that will guarantee your success.

WHERE TO LOOK FOR TEMP JOB ORDERS

Your current temporary and permanent clients. We know it's a lot easier to sell to an existing client than to a brand new client. A new client also takes time to convert, particularly in the case of temps, as it's more of a risk for the client. With permanent positions, the client can compare your candidates to another agency's by interviewing them for the same job. This enables them to compare not only the quality and suitability of the candidates, but also your service level. For temps, only one agency gets to fill a job, so when they 'try' you, they are taking a risk. My experience is you need on average five or six touch points or contacts with a client to build up enough trust for them to give you a temp job. The bigger the usage, i.e. the dollar spend of the account, the longer it takes to convert them – most key accounts have taken me six to nine months to convert. But when they do, you suddenly have lots of hours with very healthy margins due to the sheer volume of work these accounts can provide.

When you take a permanent job order. In this situation, ask if they need a temp in the meantime, so they don't have to rush to hire someone in a certain timeframe. Always ask the client if they want the best person available for a job rather than the first available person. In reality, for a permanent position most clients want to hire someone who is already in the workforce, which means the candidate will have a notice period that needs to be honoured before they can start with the client company. Yet some companies will still attempt to hire a replacement person to cross train with the outgoing person. A better solution would be for you to offer a temp who can be cross trained by the incumbent person and who can fill in until the permanent replacement is identified and then train the new employee. This gives the client a better chance of securing the *best* person.

Remember that as a 'consultant' your job is to consult, which means giving clients sound business advice that will serve them in the long run. You will find that being a trusted advisor is an excellent basis for building a business partnership, rather than being the transactional recruiter, who is only there to put someone into a position. Transactional recruiters are no longer (if they ever were) valued by clients and it is increasingly difficult for them to justify their fees. Consider that what the clients are paying you for is really your expertise in all matters recruitment.

Ask if temp-to-perm is an option. Usually your temp will have a better chance of getting the job as they get to display what they can do on the job. Even if you don't get the temp-to-perm placement, you are still more likely to get your candidates interviewed as you will be in more frequent contact with the client than other agencies, if you adopt my suggested best practice service to clients as outlined in chapter 11.

Your client's competitors. Say you deal with one telco. It is very easy to call other telcos to offer your services as you already have knowledge of their industry and more than likely temps with telco experience and skills. This is also an excellent way to build your personal brand, if working for a generalist agency. As I dealt with the two largest electronics companies in Australia, I started attracting people with electronics experience, which then made it a lot easier for me to market to other electronics companies. Inadvertently I became the 'go-to' electronics consultant for clients, temps and candidates.

Your competitor's clients. As mentioned above, reference checks can help you discover if companies use temps. Your best source of information is the people you interview. Ask where they've worked, whom you can call for reference checks and whether it was a good place to work. Just like with perms, it's far preferable for you to place your temps with reputable companies boasting good working conditions.

CASE STUDY: *Merck, Sharp & Dohme*

Back when I started in recruitment in 1990, I was told to make 30 calls a day and call every client on a fortnightly roster. One of the companies I called was Merck, Sharp & Dohme (MSD), one of the four largest pharmaceutical companies in the world. The reason I called them was that the market was very tight, with high unemployment and many redundancies. I had to go where I knew there was temp business. At MSD, an American-owned company, they had many temps on site *and* they had had the same agency supplying them for roughly ten years.

I called the HR co-ordinator, who was always polite and professional towards me; we'd have a pleasant enough chat but essentially I wasn't getting anywhere. I couldn't get to speak to one of the HR managers, I didn't get any job orders and there was no real prospect for me to get any business despite phoning every single fortnight for about seven months. What was I to do?

One late Friday night in the office after everyone else had left, I pondered whether it was time I stopped calling MSD and replaced them with another company where I might actually be able to convert the client.

Yet it seemed such a waste to stop after so much consistent effort. I looked up the *Who's Who*, which is an annually updated print reference book that tells you who all the important people are in a company. I looked up the name of the Managing Director for MSD in Australia and decided to call him. It was 6.30pm on a Friday night and much to my surprise when I asked for the MD by name, I was put straight through to him! It was so easy, yet also terrifying as I was still a relatively new consultant. We had a chat and he asked me nicely, but directly: 'What is it you want?' Excellent question, to which I answered: 'Well, I was wondering how you know you're still getting the best people and the best service at the best price, when you haven't used any other agency for ten years?' There was a pause and he said: 'You have a point, but you know I have people who look after HR for me. Can you call on Monday and speak to one of the HR managers?', and gave me the person's name.

I was absolutely over the moon ... after seven months of getting nowhere, I might finally be on my way. I called bright and early on the following Monday morning and the HR manager said before I had finished introducing myself, 'Oh you're the one who called our MD on Friday night ... what were you thinking?' We chatted for a while and then *he* asked what I wanted. I said I just wanted a 20-minute meeting to discuss his temporary staffing needs.

As I was leaving his office after the visit, we passed by the HR co-ordinator, whom he asked to give me the next job order so they could try us out! So exciting; the fact that it took another four weeks to actually get the job and that the job was apparently a 'difficult' one did not deter me at all. It was the beginning of a mutually fruitful business relationship.

Lessons I learnt from calling MSD:

- When marketing, always go straight to the top. It doesn't matter if the person you call doesn't do the actual recruitment. If he or she says: 'call Joe Blow', then Joe Blow will take your call *and* listen to what you have to say because you've spoken to his boss or even his boss's boss! This can save you a lot of time in the long run. It might save you seven months of your life...the time it took me to learn this lesson.
- Call after hours if you want to get hold of high level people, as the

receptionists and PAs will have gone home. Interestingly the person that put me through to the MD was the actual gatekeeper, i.e. the guy that raises the boom gate to their site. That was his job. His job wasn't to screen phone calls like the people we normally understand to be 'gatekeepers', i.e. receptionists and PAs.

- People in high level positions are on the whole professional and less likely to be rude or hang up on you. After all, I don't think one gets to MD-level at MSD without being professional. This means that you will get a more considered response to your calls, if not necessarily a warmer one.
- Special events create opportunities. For example, during the Queensland floods of 2011, insurance companies were inundated with customers wanting to lodge claims, hence the need for temps skyrocketed. If you hear a bank's computer system has gone down, the same applies. Constantly keep abreast of what's happening in the news. As a consultant you are a professional and need to have current business and industry knowledge. Keep up with the news in general and the business news in particular.
- Special peak times also create opportunities. For example, if it's coming up to financial year end, many companies want to have a major push on debt collections, so they have fewer liabilities. Call all your clients and offer them a collections officer. If it's approaching school holidays, ask your clients whether they have employees who are parents going on leave, as they may need temp cover. Call in advance of Melbourne Cup day and ask if they will be having a function and need phone cover. There are many more: become the clients' solution provider before they even have a problem. It's even better if you already have a temp in mind and can float that temp while asking them if they have a need. Make it easy for them to buy! Best of all is if you have a temp they've used before and loved, who is available to go back to the same company. It saves the company training time, it's easier for your temps and for you. It also demonstrates to the client that you have their interests in mind as you offer them the same temp back.

MARKETING TEMP SERVICES

How do we sell temps or any other recruitment services for that matter? Some ways are to ask for referrals from existing clients, blogging to showcase your expertise, tendering proposals – or simply making contact with a company to ask how they go about recruiting for temps. When you're starting out and when you're building your hours, you really need to be making contact with potential clients or prospects. Some recruiters and recruitment trainers say you shouldn't be calling potential clients to market your services as they consider cold calling a demeaning way to acquire new business, but I'm of the opinion that if there's someone you'd love to deal with, then the quickest way of establishing contact with that company is to make the contact yourself. Of course you need to make the call interesting for them and to engage them from the beginning. I'll cover how to do just that in this chapter.

Statistically we know it takes on average between four and seven contacts (touch points) before someone will buy from us, unless they are a referral. In my experience in the recruitment industry, it actually seems to be an average of five to six contacts. That doesn't mean that I haven't gotten a job order on the first phone call; I have. But I put that down to good timing more than anything else (sometimes I knew they had a vacancy before I made the call). It also doesn't mean that it hasn't taken me a lot more touch points to crack some major accounts. The biggest accounts took me six to nine months to crack. What made them major accounts was the fact that they already used lots of temps from a well-established competitor agency. As mentioned earlier, when you want to persuade a company to switch from a tried and tested agency to you it's a *big* risk in their eyes, and therefore it takes time to build enough trust.

Thinking about the average number of touch points before we convert a temp client, the flow from start to finish might look like this:

1. touch point – introductory call

2. touch point – handwritten card with business card attached to follow up initial phone call

3. touch point – another phone call/email

4. touch point – client visit using the consultative sales approach and *asking* for the business

5. touch point – follow up phone call

6. touch point – email/phone call/SMS

Each touch point is about building trust, finding out about your prospect's needs and challenges, and displaying your expertise and professionalism until the client feels comfortable enough to give you an opportunity. When that opportunity comes, you must be ready with excellent temps available and must service your client efficiently and effectively.

Important points to remember before you pick up the phone

When calling companies to offer your services, there are a number of important things to remember:

1. It's never about *you* when you're selling, but *always* about your client. So do not start with a sales spiel where you ramble on about who you are and what you do. The clients simply don't care. Theodore Roosevelt said: 'No one cares how much you know, until they know how much you care.'

2. Some people say you should never cold call, so let me be clear on my definition of a cold call. A cold call is simply the *first* time I speak to a client. For example, I may have been dealing with a company for a while and a new hiring manager starts. The first time I call her is a cold call for me even though I know the company very well. I may get a referral to someone and even though there is a reason for the call, it's still the *first* time I speak to that particular person, so I define it as a cold call. It's impossible to build a desk and grow your hours if you only speak to people you already know!

3. While it may be the first time you speak to someone, you can still emphasise whatever connection there is to make the call more interesting for the person on the other end. In my experience you have the initial 45-60 seconds to grab their attention: this seems to be the timeframe in which the client will decide whether or not they want to engage in conversation with you. My opening line is often like this: 'I'm calling you for two reasons. One reason is that I deal with your major competitor and in the process of interviewing for them, candidates have enquired about your company. The other reason is I noticed you just launched an exciting new product.' Naturally you have to think of two reasons that are relevant to their company, but the power in this opening is that it's about them and you don't sound like you're calling them as one of 30 companies on your call list for the day. This is a way of making them feel *special*. Refer to Roosevelt's quote.

4. Have purpose: why are you calling? If you don't know or you're doing it for the sake of meeting your KPIs, the prospect can tell that you're underprepared and that you're there for *you* and not them. Also, as the call is your initiative, you need to be steering the agenda. Don't ramble on, as this shows lack of respect for the prospect's time as well as your own.

5. Devise a wish list. When you were little, did you write a wish list for Santa? Did you have your list in descending order of the size or value of the wish? If so, you know exactly what I mean! You need to have a list of desired outcomes for each call (and visit for that matter).

The question to ask yourself is: 'If you could have anything you want from a client marketing call, what would it be, and if you can't get the biggest wish, what's your next wish?'

My wish list had five things on it:

- job order
- client visit
- referrals to other hiring contacts

- more information about their hiring intentions, what else they have planned, etc.
- for them to say 'thank you' to me for calling them

My old boss taught me that last one. Once this came onto my wish list the quality of my calls changed, as the only way I could get someone to appreciate me calling them was to give them 'value' on the call. Value meant I had to become expert in their company, industry, and in the economy so I could not only hold a business conversation, but also with any luck tell them something they didn't already know. One time a client said to me: 'The only time I find out anything about what's going on in our company is when you call'! In the age of Google alerts, it's so incredibly easy to be notified of news on any topics, keywords or company names that you want to know about. How it works is whenever Google finds a new article containing the keywords, you get an email alert with a link. There is simply *no* excuse for not being commercially aware now.

Some helpful conversation starters and useful questions

With the first point above in mind, you need to be enquiring with a curious mind when you make the initial call. Use open-ended questions that start with 'how', 'what', 'when' and 'who', but use 'why' cautiously as it can be misconstrued as you questioning their right to choose. A softer and more effective way of asking 'why' is 'May I ask why you choose to do it that way?' Open-ended questions can't be answered with a 'yes' or 'no', so they are useful for engaging the prospect and fact finding about the prospect's challenges and buying preferences. Closed questions will quickly cut off any real chance of a conversation. If you ask 'Do you use temps?' and they say 'no', the door is closed, and while you *can* prise it open again, it's better not to shut it in the first place.

Here are some useful open-ended questions for new calls:

- Are you the right person to speak to regarding the hiring of...?
- How do you generally go about it?

- How do you normally cover for holiday and sick leave? What about extended leave, e.g. maternity leave or long service leave?
- (If they use agencies) How do you decide which agency to use?
- How do you find the temps and the service that the agency offers?
- What do you like about your current providers?
- What have you disliked about their service?
- Are there any other decision makers besides yourself?
- Who else might benefit from my service?
- When is a good time for us to meet?

Notice how the aim here is to get them to talk, show interest in them and also gain information about what they look for, so you can market your features and benefits appropriately.

Closed questions are also useful when you are ready to 'close', which means to get agreement to something. For example:

- 'If you have a permanent vacancy, would you use a temp during the hiring process to give yourself plenty of time to find the right candidate?' We want to 'close' on them agreeing to use a temp and possibly extend the time to find a permanent employee, if required.
- 'Next time you need a temp, do you feel comfortable enough with me and our company to give that job to us?' Here you're going for a straight 'yes' or 'no' answer so you know where you stand.

CASE STUDY: *LG Electronics*

The first time I called LG Electronics, they had rebranded from Goldstar to LG and were really exploding onto the Australian market. The HR manager sighed and asked me when I introduced myself: 'You're a recruiter and you want to know how we recruit, right?' It was clear that she had taken many calls from other recruiters trying to elicit business! Essentially, yes, I did want to know how they recruited, but I knew I had to present a good reason for her to want to continue that conversation with me. You have to empathise with HR people who often have to take scores of phone calls from recruiters who are just in it for a quick transaction and fee. Also many unskilled recruiters will focus on themselves and how great they are, which is a complete anathema to clients.

This is what I replied: 'Actually I'm calling you for two reasons. Firstly I deal with your major competitor and in the process of interviewing for them, candidates have asked me about your company as well. Secondly I've noticed all the sexy advertising you've been doing lately on TV.' This basically opened up the conversation as there was something in it for her to speak with me about, i.e. potential experienced electronics staff. Plus I find that clients are always interested in speaking with you if you deal with their competitors. It may be just out of curiosity, or there could be an element of FOMO (fear of missing out).

The comment about their TV advertising was more about paying them a compliment and showing that their marketing efforts were working. Clients are always interested in feedback about the perception of their brand in the marketplace. Similarly, humour can be a good tactic: if you can make someone laugh, then you've managed to create instant rapport.

What happened next I put down to timing, as at the end of that conversation, I got three permanent job orders. I want to be clear that getting a job order on a first call is definitely a bonus, but wasn't the real aim of my call. If you are into transactional recruitment where you get a job, place it and then move on, then that would be *the* reason for the call.

Recruitment has evolved much over the 24 years since I started out, and the transactional model is almost extinct. I know this from my workshops with recruiters who had been operating from this model and who are now struggling as clients want much more value. Many companies have in recent years moved towards having internal talent acquisition (TA) teams, as online platforms have made it easier for them to recruit themselves. While these TA teams predominantly recruit for permanent positions, there has been an increase in them hiring their own casuals and contractors as well.

As recruiters, we must build relationships with clients and truly understand their businesses, so we can proactively advise clients on how they can recruit better-quality people while enhancing their brand in the employee market. The advantage of doing this is the clients will regard you as the 'expert' and in my experience, if you come up with the idea or solution, you will get to deliver it as well. It's unlikely that they will get one of your competitors to deliver a brainchild of yours.

Summary

- Calling your clients' competitors is an easy way to create relevance when you phone.
- You might as well use the industry knowledge and temps you already have by making that industry your area of expertise.
- Be interested in the client, their job, their company and their challenges.
- Be interesting to the client you are phoning.
- Be interested *and* interesting; if you can only be one, always choose 'be interested' as it's always about them first.
- A compliment goes a long way, as does humour.

CASE STUDY: *David Jones*

Here is an example of defining a 'problem' the client didn't even know they had. I had been dealing with David Jones for a couple of Christmases supplying them with door men. You may know these door men, who for the month of December open the door for you at the flagship stores in their grey top hats and coats on a red carpet. When I enquired as to how they recruited the rest of their temps, I was surprised to find that each store used a multitude of agencies for temps on the dock and in store. Each store manager had their own way of recruiting. I contacted the procurement officer in charge of recruitment of staff and suggested that I knew how the group could save money.

It's always important to understand the person you're dealing with and what their specific job is. In procurement the job is to source the best price, which is why I used that particular opening when I contacted them. HR's job is to source the best people, so if my call had been to HR, I would have focussed more on how I could get them better-quality people across the board, so their culture would remain intact or be further enhanced.

I was also fortunate with my timing as David Jones had recently had a new CEO appointed who had tasked procurement with re-examining the prices they were paying for various items. This edict led to them replacing the shopping-bag supplier they had dealt with for umpteen years, as they were no longer the most competitive in their pricing.

It was into this environment that I called procurement, which likely made them more receptive. A meeting was set up and I went to speak with procurement and explained that as they were using a multitude of agencies nationally, they couldn't control the quality of service and temps provided. And more importantly they weren't getting the advantage of using their considerable buying power. An example I use is: if you go into a hotel and want a room for one night, you have to pay whatever they want to charge you. However if you go into the hotel and say, 'I am after a deal for myself and 20 of my colleagues, who will use your hotel once a quarter', you will get a discount simply by combining your buying power. It becomes in the hotel's interest to give you a more attractive deal, or one of their competitors might and they'll miss out altogether.

Procurement asked me what I would suggest, and I said they should put out a tender and see what services and prices it might attract for supplying them with temps. The meeting ended with them saying they would consider my suggestion.

A few weeks later I received an invitation to tender for their temp services nationally. The good news was that I was invited to tender. The problem was that I was general manager for a boutique recruitment agency operating out of one office in Parramatta, clearly unable to provide temps nationally from a practical perspective.

I called procurement and asked if they would consider awarding the tender by state, as I was confident we could service NSW. He replied no, as they had found my arguments for going down this track compelling and convincing. They really wanted a national agency to get the most out of combining their buying power!

It looked like I might have shot myself in the foot and set up a fantastic opportunity for one of the big agencies. Fortunately for me, my director suggested I call one of the executive directors of Chandler Macleod Group. I called him and asked if they would consider subcontracting to us (i.e. supplying temps to us that we could on-supply to David Jones). Being one of the big agencies, it seemed unlikely that they would agree to do this, as they could simply tender for the contract themselves with an excellent chance of winning due to their reputation. But much to my delight, he agreed! That's how I was able to win the contract to supply David Jones with temp staff nationally.

Something I've noticed about the recruitment industry is that we isolate ourselves and are rarely inclined to work with our competitors. This seems to stem from a fear of our competitors 'stealing' our clients. My view has always been that if you can take my clients, then you deserve them as I obviously wasn't looking after them well enough. The pay-off for the industry of working together is far greater than the perceived dangers. In my David Jones experience, it is clear to me that I would not have secured that contract had we not partnered with another agency. That's business we would not have had if we'd been too afraid of working with someone else or even asking them. It's preferable to get a smaller chunk of something big than get a whole chunk of nothing! When I could add David Jones to our client list, it undoubtedly opened other doors for us as well. As an interesting postscript; every contact we dealt with at David Jones was completely delightful. Their strong customer service culture extended not only to their customers, but also their business partners.

Summary

- Do not wait for your client to have a problem; use your expertise to identify and solve problems and you will usually get to deliver the solution.
- Open your mind to collaborating with other agencies to get more hours!

THE BENEFITS OF USING TEMPS

You need to be fully conversant with the benefits to clients of using temps, as these become your sales vocabulary. Some sales people only talk about features, e.g. 'we are the largest agency in the world', yet we know that people buy benefits.

ıt doesn't really care that you have a large database, but they will ıave temps on that database with skills in their industry, package which is the benefit to them.

s are something that your service has or does, e.g. skills testing is sometning that you do.

Benefits are the result the client can expect from that particular feature, e.g. you can guarantee that the temp can actually do what they say they can do as you've tested them.

An easy way of remembering the difference between features and benefits is to say: 'what we have is skills testing of all our temp staff [feature], what that means for you is that you get the best skills match available for your needs [benefit]'. You can use this as a template until you're completely comfortable with selling benefits:

'What we have is... [feature], what that means for you is... [benefit].'

Some benefits of using temps include:

- The client only pays for the time the temp works so it's more cost effective than a permanent employee, where they have to pay for sick days, holiday pay, lunch hours etc.
- There is less administration (therefore again it is more cost effective) as the client will get one invoice, rather than having to be conversant with the correct award, issue a pay slip, calculate tax, pay the ATO, administer superannuation, pay payroll tax and any other relevant statutory costs.
- 'Try before you buy' applies in a temp-to-perm situation. The client and temp can try each other out to see if it might be a good permanent match.
- Temps can be used to cope with increased sales or workload during a permanent headcount freeze by companies who do not include temps in their headcount.
- During uncertain economic times, e.g. during the recession in the 1990s and the GFC in 2008, companies can still run their businesses without the overhead of having permanent staff on their payroll. If things get tough, they can let the temps go without redundancy payments and in many cases with only an hour's notice (provided

they have worked their day or shift minimum according to their relevant award, if applicable).

- During peak times companies can quickly hire staff as and when they need to, and possibly even re-hire the same temps back when the need arises again.
- Covering leave means that staff don't come back to an increased workload that would defeat the purpose of the leave. We saw in the 1990s that companies were retrenching so close to the bone that they suddenly saw sick days increase in their remaining staff due to stress and overwork, which cost them more time and money in the long run than if they had used temps to help out the permanent staff.
- There is a pool of skilled people available at short notice to cover for high stress areas, e.g. call centres where the absenteeism rate is high. Clients can make one call to the agency and replace their perm staff with temps for the duration of the sick leave. To value add for a client, I would have a number of temps already trained and inducted into their call centre's procedures. This makes it easier for the client to get temps working quickly and also makes it harder for your competitors to get the job order as their temps won't be trained up.
- Staff management is done by the consultant. If you give the clients top service, then they don't have to worry about absenteeism, holidays and other small issues that arise and have to be dealt with. This is part of the service and what the client pays you for: saving time, effort and money. A number of clients would let their staff call me to tell me they weren't going to be in, and I would immediately organise a replacement temp before I advised the client of the roster for the day. Effectively the client gains an extra HR employee in you, whom they only pay through temp wages. This is excellent value for money for the clients.
- Continuous coverage without any downtime or loss of productivity, which saves the client money. If you offer an after-hours service, the client can call you and get a temp to start by the time their employee normally starts.

OVERCOMING CLIENT OBJECTIONS

If you are new to the recruitment industry or lacking confidence in sales, it can appear that there are an infinite number of objections a client can come up with when you market temp recruitment services to them. But after doing more than 10,000 hours of cold calling and telemarketing, I can confidently say that all main objections can be grouped under the following three headings:

Cost: 'You're too expensive'

Competitor: 'We use another agency that we're happy with.', 'We do all our own recruitment.', 'We have a PSA (preferred supplier agreement)'

Credibility: 'We don't know if you are any good'

From a confidence and comfort point of view, I found it a lot easier once I realised that objections can be grouped like this. Once I had some different ways of overcoming each category, my confidence in picking up the phone not only soared, but I actually enjoyed making the calls! It had gone from a dreaded necessity to something I saw as a personal challenge and a bit of fun! It came down to knowing what to expect and being as prepared as I could be.

Below are some ways of overcoming the three types of objections.

Cost: You're too expensive

When a client says 'you're too expensive', they want to drag you into a 'dollars and cents' conversation, which only looks at the hourly rate charged. On the face of it, your rate may be higher than your competitor's, but is it actually more expensive? Remember a temp is usually called in to perform a specific task. The more efficiently and effectively this is done, the better *value* for the client. A 'cheaper' temp may be slower, less accurate, less proficient, which means they will take more hours to do the same job. They or someone else will have to spend time going back over the work to check it for accuracy. Someone will most likely have to spend more time showing them what to do, which takes that person away from their own job, for which there's a measurable cost as well. This is clearly false economy for the client.

If they've previously had a temp with poor skills, they will not need to be convinced of the false economy. They may instead wonder how your temps are going to be different, which is really our third objection, 'How do I know you are you any good at your job?', which is about your credibility as a consultant. Understandably a client who has been burnt will be harder to convince to use a temp again.

Another scenario is that when clients are used to getting second-rate temps, they may not even know what they can get in terms of competency and professionalism from a temp, as they think they are already getting the best available.

A good starting point when a client says: 'You're too expensive' is for you to ask 'Compared to what?' We all know that if we buy a dress from Target or Prada that there will be a difference in price. One is not necessarily better than the other; just different. Likewise you can choose to be the Target or Prada of your niche in recruitment. But it is important that you make a conscious business decision. Imagine how confusing it would be for the client if they went to Target and had to pay Prada prices. So the 'Compared to what?' question is to ensure that your client is comparing apples with apples. As we are in a service industry, it is vital to focus on the service and value you provide when a comparison is being made. As you have tested your temps' skills, you know exactly what the client is paying for. As some agencies do not do skills testing, this provides for an unequal comparison.

Example: Your client may have a data entry assignment and been quoted $38.00 per hour and you may quote $41.74 per hour. On the face of it, the other agency looks cheaper but they may be sending someone at 8000 keystrokes per hour with 90% accuracy, whereas you're sending someone at 18,000 keystrokes with 99% accuracy. Chances are that your temp will do the job in half the time and as the client only pays for the time the temp works, they have in fact saved money by using your temp at the higher rate. Also if you've provided them with a 20-minute call back service, then they've received better service as well as a better temp for less money. The better service equates to peace of mind for them as they know a temp is booked and they can concentrate on doing their own job rather than worrying about whether a temp is available. Always ask what they are comparing your price to and what they are getting for it.

CASE STUDY: *Samsung Electronics*

Years ago I was marketing to Samsung Electronics and after calling them fortnightly for nine months with no result, the HR manager called out of the blue with a data-entry job order! He told me plainly that this was my one and only chance to prove myself to them. I sent him a temp, who did the job in half the allotted time at 100% accuracy. When I called to do the four-hour check, she had already finished the work! This was a memorable start to a long and mutually satisfying business partnership. Samsung became a major account for our entire company of 30 branches.

Lessons I learnt from Samsung:

- Persistence really does pay off. By phoning every fortnight like clockwork, the time when Samsung needed a temp did come around. You stay at the forefront of your client's mind when you are in contact regardless of whether they have any needs.
- When you finally get an opportunity to supply, send them your best! If you don't have someone good enough on the day, be brave and tell your client that you can't help. On the occasions I've had to do this, clients have always come back to me. They appreciate the honesty and integrity you display by not sending them someone rather than just sending them anyone and hoping for the best. Sometimes the clients had experienced another agency assuring them they had the right temp when in fact they didn't, and they realised that the agency was substandard as well as the temp. Sending your clients elsewhere may sound scary, but if you're giving best practice service then it usually only serves to highlight just how good your service is!
- Do not oversell your temp's skills. Just be factual about what they tested at. In the Samsung example, I knew how good she was, but just gave the manager the facts about her speed and accuracy when I booked her in. This allowed her to pleasantly surprise him and provided the opportunity to create a raving fan.

Competitor:
a) We use another agency we're happy with

My approach to this is: 'I'm so pleased to hear that you're experiencing good service. It's good to know that there are other professional people out there upholding the reputation of our industry. May I ask what it is in particular you like about your current supplier?' The specificity of their answers is critical as the client will tell you what they value in a temp service. Listen and note their answer without commenting. Then ask: 'Is there anything that they don't do, that you wish they did?'

Again listen carefully. Once they have told you what they like *and* dislike, you can jump in with your relevant features and benefits that specifically address what they value.

The client might say: 'I really like that they always get back to me within a day of my placing a temp job order with them. Plus they also offer a good guarantee if the temp doesn't work out.'

It's critical that you listen carefully as the client is telling you what matters to them. This information sets you up nicely to highlight your service features and the attached benefits.

My reply: 'Actually if speed and peace of mind is important to you, then you might like to know that we offer a 20-minute call back service, which means that within 20 minutes of your call, we will confirm the name of the temp with you.'

If the client highlights your competitor guarantee and you know your guarantee is better, you can say: 'In terms of guarantee, our guarantee is that if you're not happy, you will get the first temp free and the replacement temp's first seven hours are free as well. As far as I know, this is the best temp guarantee in the business. Honestly, we would be out of business if clients had to call on our guarantee often, so we work very hard to ensure that we get it right the first time. Seeing you mentioned the temp guarantee, is it something you've had to call upon quite a bit?'

You have to realise that when a client says, 'we're happy' or 'we have a PSA', or anything like that, it's often to get you off the phone. What I call a fob off. So it pays to dig a bit deeper. Your job is to understand your client's needs and concerns; ask questions to show interest and find out what's important to the them.

Another way to tackle the fact that they already have an agency is to say: 'From time to time, if your supplier doesn't have the right person available, perhaps you'd like to give us a try? As we don't have temps waiting on a shelf, it can happen to the best of us that the skill you need on a particular day isn't readily available. How do you feel about using us as your back-up agency in a situation like that?'

Competitor:
b) We do all our own recruitment

When this objection is raised, some probing questions are good to find out a bit more. You can use a little preamble: 'That's great that you have in-house capacity to fill your own jobs.'

- 'Out of interest; how often do you have to call a casual in?'
- 'How many phone calls do you normally have to make to fill a shift or assignment?'
- 'What happens if none of your ex-employees or pool of casuals are available when you need them?'
- 'How would you fill the vacancy then?'
- 'Do you have an agency you use in that circumstance?'
- 'Would you consider using us?'

Competitor:
c) We have a PSA (preferred supplier agreement)

In this case, ask the following:

- 'What type of staff does your PSA cover?' Usually PSAs only cover perms or temps. Or they may be for a certain type of staff, e.g. accounting, while all other types of staff can be recruited from anywhere and anyone. If the PSA doesn't cover what you provide, then you can fill a gap, so proceed with your call as normal.

- 'Is it an official or unofficial agreement? If official, is it usually by invitation to tender or is it a public tender? When is it due for renewal? How can we get invited to tender as well?'

Again this is about you asking intelligent, probing questions, which has the added side-effects of showing interest in them and of displaying your industry knowledge, so you can find an opening to discuss your service features and benefits. Or at least find out when a tender opportunity may be available. If the tender renewal is 9-12 months out, it's actually an ideal time for you to establish and build on some contacts in the company. At least you won't be a completely unknown entity to the company when the time comes for tendering.

You may even consider offering a free temp for a week or a shorter timeframe to one of the contacts you cultivate. This may be enough to get you an invitation to tender when the time comes around for renewal of the tendering agreement as your company will be on record as having provided a temp in the past. Presumably you will also be able to provide an internal client testimonial from the grateful client who got the free temp! Whilst this strategy may cost you a week's temp wages, it's a relatively small investment to make to have a decent chance at securing a major PSA which may be worth thousands, if not millions of dollars.

Also ask if you can provide them with temps if ever the suppliers on their PSA can't supply. Often this is the case, as PSA rates may be so low that well-qualified people are unwilling to fill the jobs, or the agency may simply not have that particular skill set available the day the client requires it. Usually this means you can supply at your normal hourly rates rather than at the rates prescribed in the agreement. Being a back-up agency can open doors for you when the tender comes around for renewal as you will have proven both the quality of your service and the quality of your temps.

CASE STUDY: *Australian Administration Services*

The first time I tendered to supply Australian Administration Services (AAS) with temps, I wasn't successful, but we became their back-up agency. During the year of that 12-month contract duration, their preferred supplier couldn't keep up with filling the orders, so we got more and more of the work thanks to our speed and the quality of temps we delivered. When the contract next went out for tender, we were in an extremely strong position as we had many successful runs on the board and had established a strong relationship with AAS managers and employees. This, I believe, was a strong contributing factor to us winning the next tender process.

Credibility: We don't know if you are any good

This is about your personal or your company's ability and credibility. A good way to overcome this objection is to use a case study or tell a story (which by the way is the most effective way of transferring information as people remember stories). It may be a story about another company in the prospect's industry, i.e. their competitor, who used to use someone else but now uses you as you were able to source the specialist employees they needed. If you have a testimonial from that company, even better!

I'm a *huge* fan of testimonials as they provide social proof that you can in fact do the job. They have always worked well, but with the prolific use of social media today, they have become even more effective as a marketing tool. Whether you like it or not, people will post, tweet and update on how you stack up.

I'm sure you have clients who literally 'love your guts'; do you have a written testimonial from them? If not, why not? With a folder of testimonials in hand, you can with confidence say to a client: 'I could tell you how good we are, but it's probably more credible for you to hear it from some of our clients. So at a time that suits you, I'd like to come and spend 20 minutes with you to give you an opportunity to tell me about how you prefer to work with a recruitment agency and you can view our testimonials at the same time. That way you can see first-hand who we deal with.'

This approach allows you to organically ask for a client visit. Notice how I don't ask in a closed question way: 'Can I show you our testimonials at a meeting?' That would more likely have elicited a 'no'. Also notice how I use the word 'you' more than the word 'I'? Remember in selling and influencing, it's not about *you*, but always about your client!

Two sales power words to use frequently are 'you' and 'yours'. Bearing this in mind also forces you to think about why it's in the client's interest to agree to what you're suggesting. Which is another way of ensuring you're focusing on the benefits for them.

Overcoming objections is a special skill set that can be learned through practice, focus and sales training. Practice is the most important aspect. In Malcolm Gladwell's *Outliers* he has many examples of how the average person with dedication to practice trumps the person who has more talent, but who does not devote the time to practice.

I know; I learnt how to overcome objections effectively by making thousands of calls and visits. I had to make 30 calls per day, which took roughly eight hours as I didn't have any jobs to fill. Forty hours per week x 48 weeks = 1920 hours per annum. It would only take five years to achieve Gladwell's 10,000 hours at that rate. In fact I did get a lot busier filling jobs once the temp desk took off, which was roughly six months after making those 30 calls a day, but after 18 years in the job, I'm sure I have devoted a lot more than 10,000 hours to marketing!

By starting your calls today, you ensure that you're well on the path to your own mastery. By using the ideas in this book, you will be able to shave off some time, but reading about them is not enough. Practice, practice, practice!

CHAPTER 8

$$ WHAT TO PAY AND CHARGE FOR TEMPS

DETERMINING YOUR PAY RATES

Temp rates are usually governed by awards or an enterprise or site agreement. Award rates are most common.

Depending on what type of temps you supply, you will have to look up the relevant award for that category.

Since the 1st of January 2010, we now have modern awards in Australia, and a list of these 122 awards can be found at www.fairwork.gov.au.

Here you can search for the award that's applicable to your temps. As I've used clerical staff as my example, I will use the Clerks Private Sector Award 2010 here for illustration. If you wish to refer to awards pre-2010, they can be found at the same website under 'pre-modern awards'.

While you may have a payroll person or company that pays your temps and invoices your clients, I believe that you need to know the basic award conditions that apply to your temps as your temps and clients will need to access this information at some point. Learning about awards and how to interpret them is one way you can provide expertise to your clients.

The Clerks Private Sector Award 2010 covers all clerical employees in Australia unless they are covered by another award specific to their industry (as listed here):

- the Aged Care Award 2010
- the Airline Operations - Ground Staff Award 2010
- the Airport Employees Award 2010
- the Alpine Resorts Award 2010
- the Animal Care and Veterinary Services Award 2010
- the Banking, Finance and Insurance Award 2010
- the Black Coal Mining Industry Award 2010
- the Business Equipment Award 2010
- the Contract Call Centres Award 2010
- the Educational Services (Post - Secondary Education) Award 2010
- the Educational Services (Schools) General Staff Award 2010
- the Fitness Industry Award 2010
- the General Retail Industry Award 2010
- the Health Professionals and Support Services Award 2010
- the Higher Education Industry – General Staff – Award 2010
- the Hospitality Industry (General) Award 2010
- the Legal Services Award 2010
- the Market and Social Research Award 2010
- the Rail Industry Award 2010
- the Restaurant Industry Award 2010
- the Sporting Organisations Award 2010
- the Telecommunications Services Award 2010.

Here are the basic things in the Clerks Private Sector Award that you need to know:

- Ordinary hours are 38 hours per week or 152 hours over 28 days.

- Ordinary hours can be worked between 7am and 7pm Monday to Friday and 7am to 12.30pm on Saturdays.
- The casual loading is 25% on the equivalent hourly rate for a permanent employee. So you need to know what the permanent weekly wage is for an adult:
  Level 1 permanent weekly wage – $661.60
  As a normal week is 38 hours, you divide $661.60 by 38 to find the hourly rate:
  $661.50 ÷ 38 = $17.41
  To determine the casual rate, you add 25% casual loading:
  $17.41 + 25% = $21.76 per hour
  This is for a Level 1 employee, which is the lowest level in this award.
- Current adult (21 years and older) casual pay rates are between $21.76 and $27.09 per hour depending on what level the temp is classified under the award.
- Shifts are a three-hour minimum, which means when you send a temp out, you must pay them for three hours even if they only work for two. This charge is passed on to your client as it's an award requirement. I would normally ask the client if they have some extra work in order to utilise the temp for the full three hours as they have to pay for them anyway.
- Overtime for work done on a Saturday is at time and one quarter (xT1¼) provided the temp has already worked 38 hours that Monday-to-Friday week. The minimum Saturday shift is three hours.
- Overtime for work done on a Sunday is at double time (xT2) with the minimum shift being four hours.
- The temp is entitled to a minimum of 10 hours off between consecutive days' work or they shall be paid at double time (xT2).
- Adults under this award are 21 years and older. If younger than 21 years they shall be paid according to their age as stipulated in the award.
- The temps are entitled to have a meal provided or a meal allowance of

$14.08, if they work more than 1.5 hours of overtime without 24 hours notice. If they work more than four hours overtime without 24 hour notice, then a further meal allowance of $11.27 is payable.

The above is correct at the time of writing and according to my interpretation of the modern award pertaining to clerks. It is your responsibility to keep up to date with award increases, which usually happen once a year. To make it easy, you can enter the relevant award name as a keyword into Google alerts and be notified whenever there's any news about that particular award.

DETERMINING A CHARGE RATE

Using our Level 1 pay rate of $21.76, we could use the following formula to work out a charge rate to the client:

pay rate + on-costs + markup = charge rate

On-costs are dependent upon where you're supplying the temps as they vary from state to state and of course from country to country.

Let's use NSW as an example. On-costs are: 9.25% superannuation, 5.45% payroll tax, 2% workers compensation (this is an average estimate as the exact rate will depend on which industry they work in). You could add 1% for professional indemnity and public liability insurances, giving you a total of:

9.25 + 5.45 + 2 + 1 = 17.7%, or you can round this up to 18% on-costs.

If you choose to use a 30% markup, then your charge rate would be:

$21.76 + 18% + 30% = $33.38 per hour per weekday

It costs you $21.76 + 18% = $25.68 to have the person out working per hour as this includes the rate paid to the temp plus all the relevant on-costs.

Your gross margin per hour would be $33.38 - $25.68 = $7.70

If that temp worked a 38-hour week, your weekly gross margin would be $292.72

I like to work on a higher markup, e.g. 40-45% which would make the charge rates look like this:

40% markup:

$21.76 + 18% + 40% = $35.95

with a gross margin of $10.27 per hour or $390.26 per week
45% markup:
$21.76 + 18% + 45% = $37.23 per hour
with a gross margin of $11.55 per hour or $438.90 per week

It's far preferable to use a formula like this than work on a fixed dollar margin. I have seen some companies adopt a fixed margin of $5.00 per hour regardless of what type of temp they supply. The problem with this is that the higher skilled temps are scarcer and therefore harder to find, which means the margin the client pays you for sourcing, attracting and managing those higher skilled temps isn't aligned with the amount of work you're investing in filling their assignment. For example, if you advertise for call-centre operators, you may get lots of applicants with varying degrees of experience. You may be able to use a large number of those with excellent work histories, as you can use your influencing skills to persuade the client to hire them on a lower or trainee level. If on the other hand your client needs a call-centre supervisor with minimum three to five years experience in the insurance industry, the search is likely to be extensive, as many of these may not be available for temp work. If you use the formula with a markup as a percentage component, then your dollar margin will be proportional to the level of temp skill required.

PAYROLLING A TEMP

On occasion clients may want you to payroll a temp or you may find that a company has a decent-size pool of their own casuals and you can offer to payroll them. Payrolling is different from supplying a temp in that the client has sourced the temp or casual that they want to hire. There can be various reasons why they prefer the casual to be on an agency's payroll, including headcount restrictions and avoiding the hassle of having to administer wages, superannuation, workers compensation and other costs. Another reason can be that they simply want the skills of the casual, but not the hassle of day-to-day management of them. The relationship that they have with the casual changes as it's no longer an employer and employee situation. The casual is hired as a temp through the agency, who then on-hires that temp to the client.

The benefits to the client of the on-hire arrangement as opposed to a direct hire arrangement are pretty clear and easy for you to 'sell' to your clients:

- The client only pays one invoice rather than being responsible for administering statutory costs as well as the temp's entitlements.
- The relationship with temp is at arm's length although there are some work health and safety (WHS) obligations.
- Management of the temp is done by the temp agency, including dealing with performance issues, hiring and firing.

What to charge for payrolling a temp

As you didn't source, recruit and present the temp to the client, but essentially are performing an administrative function for the client, the charge rate may be worked out differently. Clients expect that the recruitment industry in Australia often charge a lower hourly rate than for a standard temp. So instead of using our formula:

pay rate + on-costs + % markup = client charge rate,

it might look more like this:

pay rate + on-costs + $5.00 = client charge rate.

For example, if the award pay rate is $21.76:

$21.76 + 18% + $5.00 = $30.68 per hour per weekday

This gives you a dollar margin of $5.00.

Depending on how you pay your temps, you can adjust the flat hourly dollar margin you add on for providing a payroll service. The lowest I've heard for a payrolling service was an hourly margin of $2.00.

If you come across a client with many of their own casuals on their books, you may want to market this service to them. If successful your hours will grow, but your average hourly margin will of course be affected. That's why it's important to focus on number of hours and average margin when growing your temp desk. We all know of recruitment companies who have 'bought' business by offering unsustainably low margins. This might be part of their strategy for winning certain employer brands as clients, but in the long term, this is not good business practice. You end up doing a lot of work for little or no return. Or you get a workers compensation claim that instantly decimates your earnings.

Some things to consider

1. While there are award rates, temps are usually paid well above those rates in a skill-short market. Temps need to be highly skilled and there is fierce competition to get the best temps. Clients need to be educated on the difference between award rates, which tell us the absolute minimum rates temps have to be paid, and market rates, which are what their skills and experience command in the current temp market.

2. Remember when I used the analogy of a Prada dress and a Target dress? Or the comparison between a Mercedes and a Toyota? One is not necessarily better than the other, but each of these brands serves a different demographic and purpose and therefore sits in a different price category. Before you decide what your percentage markup is, think about the temporary recruitment industry and where you want to pitch your temp service. Are you the Mercedes or the Toyota of temp agency providers?

3. Never compete on price, i.e. dollars and cents; it's a race to the bottom of the lowest, untenable margins and lowers the service levels in the industry. Always compete on value. With 'value' in mind, this is how you decide where you want to pitch your temp services.

4. If you also provide a permanent placement or other complementary recruitment services, then your temp service offering needs to be aligned to them. So if you offer top-of-the-line permanent recruitment services at 20-25% fees, then your temp hourly charge rates should also be in the higher range, ie 45-50% markup. Incidentally I have always been amongst the most expensive in terms of temp hourly rates. My rationale for this:

- We had the best temps as the benchmarks were set high for people wanting to temp for us in terms of hard, measurable skills.
- Our service was the best: 20-minute call back service, treating clients with honesty and integrity.
- We had the best temp guarantee in the business, so there was no risk to the clients.
- My experience tells me unequivocally that clients do not complain about the rates, if they are happy with the temp and your service. They *only* complain if you give them $2-shop value and charge them top dollar. So if you decide to charge them top dollar, make sure your service and temps cannot be faulted!

5. If a client asks you for a discount, please re-read the chapter about overcoming objections, specifically the cost/price objection. One good way of growing your hours is to ask the client how much temp business they have, as you'd consider a 'bulk' discount like in the David Jones example. Think very carefully about giving them a discount without blinking, as it's nearly impossible to raise your rates again unless you change your service offering to include a lot more 'value'.

6. Consider how much margin you're prepared to do payrolling for. Why do you want to do it? Is it to get a foot in the door of that particular client company, so you can supply them with other more lucrative recruitment services?

BUSINESS PARTNERSHIP OR MASTER-SERVANT RELATIONSHIP?

When dealing with a client, it's critical that you learn to get comfortable with discussing rates. Every time you confirm a temp, you need to confirm the rate verbally and in an email. Upon booking you will say, for example: 'I've booked Julia for you and the rate for her is $38.98 per hour per weekday up to 38 hours per week or 7.6 hours per day. For anything after this overtime applies as per the Clerks Private Sector Award 2010. She will bring a time sheet with her or you can access our online time sheet to verify her hours on a weekly basis, so we can pay her correctly and invoice you accordingly. The verified time sheet needs to be with us by 10am on Monday mornings.'

Again the more specific you are in setting expectations, the fewer problems will appear later on. If you rely on your client to read an email with your hourly rate, then this can easily fall through the cracks. The client can claim she didn't have time to read it, or she would have raised the issue of the hourly rate with you. It's extremely messy to discuss rates once a temp has already started on their assignment as you're bound by the rate quoted to the temp. As you are the expert in the temporary recruitment field, you must be confident of your abilities and 'stand up' for your rates and service. Imagine if we went to a medical specialist and said: 'No, I don't agree with your diagnosis and I think your fee is unreasonable'! This is unthinkable, as we simply accept that they are the experts and it's just not the type of service that people negotiate on.

Having said that, there may be situations where you actually *want* to negotiate with a client, e.g. if they use multiple temps and you want a bigger slice of their business. In this case, ask them what their usage is in terms of dollar spend, temp numbers, type of temps and most importantly whether they are willing to give you this business.

Once you have this information, you can make an informed decision around what you're prepared to sacrifice in percentage markup to gain the extra hours. Most importantly remember that in negotiations, it's give and take from both parties. If the client doesn't give you anything in the form of information or more temp job orders, *but* you agree to give them a lower hourly rate, the previously equal business relationship has suddenly turned into a master-servant relationship. They command and you respond by jumping however high they want you to jump. Not only have you lost money as you've had to lower your margin, but also your credibility; if you don't believe in and fight for your rates, then why would the client?

The way we think about our jobs and our roles will in turn determine our behaviour, which can be a strength or a weakness.

Example

A new client calls you with your very first job order. When you call to book the temp in and quote the rate, the client tells you that it's too high and they want a $2.00 discount.

What are your options here?

1. You can reduce your margin to secure the job.

2. You can explain that your rate is determined by market rates and you've booked them Joe with x, y, z skills.

3. You can ask for a meeting to gather information about their total temp usage, so you can give them preferential rates for exclusivity.

4. You can offer them David at the $2.00 lower rate, but explain carefully the difference in David's and Joe's skills, e.g. David may have less experience in that particular skill set and therefore may take slightly longer to complete the work. Explain that David commands a lower hourly rate, which is what enables you to offer him out at the cheaper charge rate. Also explain that you would never try to underpay Joe according to market rates as this may cause resentment and prevent him from agreeing to work for your client next time.

As per your policy, you always book the best person available, but if your client insists on having a say in the rate charged, then let her decide which temp she wants. Most clients will actually choose the more expensive person when they understand the difference in skill set. When it comes down to actual real people rather than just speaking theoretically about skill levels the client's understanding shoots up.

The conversation always needs to be about value and not dollars and cents. I consider that a big part of a recruiter's job is to educate clients on market conditions. After all it's your expertise, not theirs; be generous with your knowledge and share what you know with your clients.

Which of the above options would you choose? I would either choose option 3) or do a combination of 4) and 3) to get this booking confirmed and then work on cementing the relationship with the client for the long term. Option 1) is really by far the worst option for you. I suspect some clients use requesting a discount as a 'test' to see how willing you are to defend your expertise. Sadly I know that many recruiters automatically say 'yes' when they are asked to drop their rates, which in turn causes them to feel resentment towards the client. In my view this situation is completely of your own choosing and making. You need to become better at trumpeting your own and your temps' strengths. You probably know the feeling yourself when you come across someone who is knowledgeable; you feel you're in good hands and you're usually willing to pay for that peace of mind.

CHAPTER 9

HOW TO PAY YOUR TEMPS AND CHARGE YOUR CLIENTS

TIME SHEETS AND PAY

The Clerks Private Sector Award provides that employees must be paid weekly or fortnightly, but as you only get paid when your temp has been paid, the most common process is to pay the temps weekly. As on-hire staff, temps don't have to adhere to the client company's pay week, so you can decide when a week starts and finishes. When I worked at Ecco, our temporary week went from Thursday to Wednesday. It was up to the temps to get their signed time sheet to us on time which was by Friday evening at 5pm. Most agencies have weeks that go from Monday to Sunday now. Whatever your week is, you have to allow enough time for the time sheet information to be collated and pays to be done in time for the payment deadline. Please check your specific award to see if there are any particular days your temps have to be paid by.

If you are supplying a contractor, i.e. someone who is being paid as a company with their own ABN, then you should be able to negotiate when they are to be paid. If they work as a sole trader, you must treat them as an on-hire staff i.e. just like a temp.

It's very important that you emphasise to the temps at their initial interview that it's their responsibility to get their time sheets authorised and forwarded to you via email, fax or hard copy by a certain time. Otherwise you may end up spending many hours chasing your temps for time sheets, which doesn't actually grow your hours and inhibits you from doing so. The only line to take on this is to say that if their time sheet isn't in, they won't get paid, but also tell them that it greatly inconveniences the client company who may have a certain budget to be spent within a certain time.

Here is a good way to ask temps to send you their authorised time sheets on time:

'Our working week goes from Monday to Sunday, but if your working week finishes on a Friday, you need to get the client to sign your time sheet or to authorise it via email, so you can get paid on time. If I don't get the time sheet by Friday 5pm, you will miss the pay run. If you need to work the weekend, then your deadline for getting the time sheet to us is by Monday morning at 10am. If your manager is away or in a meeting, then call me on Friday and let me know, so I can get authorisation from someone else, so you can get paid. If your assignment finishes on a different day to Friday, then make sure you get your approved time sheet to me before you leave the company.'

Most recruitment companies pay their temps first and then invoice their clients with a copy of the approved time sheet attached. If you don't get the time sheet on time, you can't pay the temp, which means you can't invoice the client, which also means you can't count those hours in your weekly billings! Therefore it's absolutely imperative that you get your temps trained to be very disciplined with getting their time sheets in on time.

Remember the successful recruiter is always juggling the three critical tasks on a daily basis. If you have to waste time chasing time sheets, then it's precious time away from the three critical tasks! I've known some consultants who spend half a day chasing time sheets – it keeps them occupied but with a totally non-productive task as the work for those hours has already been done and it doesn't directly generate any more hours.

As a temp consultant you walk a very fine line between being your temps' boss and confidante, but you can't get too chummy with them as they won't respect you which means they won't do what you need them to do at the times you need them to.

Also remember that *specificity is gold.* Be specific when you ask for something, e.g. say: 'Please have your time sheet to me by 5pm. If you can't, then let me know by 5pm.' It's far more precise than saying: 'Get your manager to sign your time sheet at the end of the day and email it to me asap.' By being specific, you leave no room for misunderstandings or excuses!

If a temp doesn't do what you expected, examine what your instructions were. Either you weren't specific enough or they aren't good at taking instruction. If the latter is the case, then you have to consider whether they are suitable to work as a temp as their job is to take instructions from various people in a multitude of assignments. You want people who can quickly grasp instructions and comply.

INVOICING CLIENTS

Invoicing a client can be done in different ways, such as:

- You may have an integrated system where you can log a job with the correct pay and charge rates and once a temp has been paid, it automatically generates an online and/or a hard copy invoice.
- You may outsource this function to an external provider, in which case they may chase the time sheet for you and invoice the clients.
- You may input your time sheet hours into MYOB or QuickBooks.

Whichever way you do it, you have to ensure the clients are invoiced immediately as your temps are already paid, which means your cash is outstanding. As clients understand you're paying the temps upfront, you can ask for seven day payment on all temp invoices. Seven days is standard procedure in the industry anyway. Be on the watch for temp invoices that don't get paid as companies in trouble have been known to use temp agencies to fund their business. When you deal with a new temp client, you must state upfront that because you pay your temps on a weekly basis, all temp invoices are payable within seven days and ask if this can be adhered to. If they say they only pay invoices in 30 days, I would add another 2% markup on the hourly rate to take this into account. If you give a client the option, they will usually go with the seven days and lower hourly rate. If you're dealing with a large company or government organisation where their accounts payable runs are fairly rigid, you may decide that you will accept different payment terms to the seven days. I would only do it for a large client, i.e. one which uses many temps at once and if I get the business exclusively. What you end up doing needs to be guided by your company policy and cash-flow situation.

FUNDING YOUR TEMP PAYROLL

Now that you know you need to pay your temps upfront before invoicing the clients, you need to decide how best to fund your temp desk. While having a temp desk is very lucrative and guaranteed money in the bank, you do need to have working capital to start one up.

Some different funding options:

- You have cash deposits which you can use for this purpose.
- You borrow money from a bank to fund your temp payroll.
- You use factoring (also known as debtor finance). This is a process where you 'sell' your invoices to a bank or financial provider for 75-80% of the invoice value. The bank or provider will then collect the money owed on the invoice and pay you the balance of the invoice value, after deducting commission and fees. If after a certain time, e.g. 30 days, the client hasn't paid, the factoring business will pay the recruitment company and start collection proceedings against the client.
- You outsource to an external service provider, who will do all back office functions including paying your temps for a percentage of your margin or a flat fee.

To determine the best option for you, you will need to get financial advice, as every business is different as is every business owner. In chapter 17, David Payne, a chartered accountant with his own business servicing the recruitment industry, talks in more detail about how to obtain funding for your growing desk.

CHAPTER 10

BEST PRACTICE SERVICE FOR TEMPS

As a temp consultant, you have two equally important client groups: 1) your temps, without whom you can't supply any client companies; and 2) your client companies, without whom you can't provide any work for your temps. When you think about your job in this way, it is obvious that *both* groups require dedication and care. I have seen recruiters treat their temps with disdain and a lack of respect, and then they wonder why the temps don't feel any loyalty towards them!

In fact, depending on the market you're in, quality temps may be harder to source and therefore be more 'valuable' than clients. If there is a shortage of talent, then finding and retaining talent becomes paramount to all employers and this includes *you* as the temp employer.

To be the best temp recruiter, you need to be able to attract temps to you, which is only the beginning. Then there is the process of earning their trust and loyalty, so they will do anything for you and be your ambassador to client companies and other temps. Every interaction you have with a temp is an opportunity to cement and deepen that relationship.

A TYPICAL CHAIN OF TEMP INTERACTIONS

1. The temp emails you their resume

All resumes ideally need to be responded to within 24 hours. If you get a walking dollar temp, they probably won't even last that long. Have you ever called a temp and they've already found work? That's because you didn't respond quickly enough or enthusiastically enough. Once a recruitment company asked me to be a 'mystery applicant' to test their company's response time. The consultant in question was even told this was to happen *and* given my real name which I used. To this day, I haven't had a response and that was about two years ago! Admittedly, I didn't display much relevant experience in my application form, but that's besides the point, or perhaps exactly the point. *Every* application needs to be responded to. If you've put out an advertisement and you're being inundated with resumes and find this process too onerous, then at the very least have a standard email response saying either:

'Thank you for your application. In this instance, you haven't been successful, but we wish you all the best in your job search. Please feel free to apply to us in future for any other vacancies.'

Or:

'Due to the high volume of responses, our aim is to get back to you within 24 hours of this email. Thank you for your interest in this position and your patience.'

I recommend that you only dedicate two time slots per day to look at and respond to your emails, e.g. at 8.30am for one hour and then again at 4.30pm for one hour. When you do, decide whether each applicant goes into your 'yes', 'no' or 'maybe' pile. Call all the 'yes' people immediately and arrange interviews with them in the next 24 hours. Send the 'thanks, but no thanks' standard response to the people in the 'no' pile. Email the 'maybe' people with the 'we will get back to you within 24 hours' response.

2. The temp comes in for interview

Naturally you will already have explained to them the format of the interview, the duration and what to expect. If you are going to be administering tests, tell them in advance, so they allow for this in their parking time. The interview is for you to establish the temp's skills and determine whether they are a good fit for your temp team in terms of the benchmarking you have put in place. If you decide you can use the temp, then you need to lay down the ground rules of what they can expect from you and likewise what you expect from them. If you can't use the temp, it's appropriate you tell them why, as it may be something they can fix. This is where the consulting part of 'temp consultant' comes in. Be generous with your expertise and actually consult. If you don't, you've chosen to be just a job filler, which is a long way from consulting.

CASE STUDY: *Amy (temp applicant)*

Years ago I had an American applicant, let's call her Amy, register with me for temp work. Amy was highly qualified and had recently been a general manager for a luxury hotel chain in the USA. Amy had almost everything: right attitude, common sense, intelligence and professionalism, but unfortunately not the word-processing package that most clients had converted to in Australia. She had WordStar, but at that time our clients were all using WordPerfect. I told Amy this and she asked if she did a course in WordPerfect whether I would be able to find her some temp work. I said: 'Absolutely', as that was the only element needed to make her a walking dollar temp.

Amy went and did the course, and I sent her as my very first temp to Merck, Sharp and Dohme (remember the MD I called late on a Friday night?). Unbeknownst to me at the time, Amy had been to another agency before she came to me. The consultant there had told her they would find her work, but she never heard from them again. It turned out it was the same agency that Merck had used for 10 years! While I don't think they set out to treat her poorly, they should have known that they couldn't place her with her WordStar skills. Rather than tell her this vital nugget of local market information, they chose to leave it, with unfortunate and lasting consequences for themselves.

Amy was such a good temp that she was kept on at Merck long past the initial booking dates. During this time, she would tell everyone that the other agency had treated her in an unprofessional way and that only I had been honest enough to tell her what she needed to upskill herself and ultimately find work. Without knowing the backstory, I had inadvertently put the best ambassador into Merck that I could have hoped for. Think about how you treat your temps and applicants as they can be your best brand ambassadors or your worst detractors. While looking after your brand has always been important, in the current climate of social media, it's critically important. People can trash a brand quicker that you can bat an eyelid.

It's easy to tell people the truth when it relates to their skill level, e.g. they aren't fast enough or advanced enough. It's more difficult when it's about something they can't change or something which they may consider to be discriminatory. In these cases, you must tread cautiously.

CASE STUDY: *Bob (candidate for a temp-to-perm position)*

One time I had an excellent call-centre operator apply for a temp-to-perm job with one of my electronics clients. Let's call him Bob. Bob had solid call-centre experience and was an outgoing, caring person – just the kind you want in your call centre. During our interview, all I could do was stare at his eyebrow ring. I knew that that particular electronics client would take one look at Bob and the client interview would be over, regardless of his skill set.

I didn't want to waste Bob's, my client's or my time, plus Bob was such a good temp that I really wanted him to work for us. At the end of the interview, I said to Bob: 'I think you're great. The only concern I have is that the manager at the company you've applied for will probably ask you to take out your eyebrow ring. I personally don't have a problem with the eyebrow ring, but if I don't give you this information, it will diminish your chances of getting that job and then I wouldn't be doing my job properly. How do you feel about that? If you'd prefer not to work there, I have another client which is a funky young credit-card company and they would warmly welcome you into their team. What do you think?' Bob thanked me for my honesty and said he was interested in the credit-card company position. As predicted, that client loved him and Bob ended up securing a permanent job there.

In my experience, you can say almost anything if it's said with sincerity and from a place of caring. What can get you into trouble is saying it in a judgemental and non-caring manner. Always make it clear that it's not your personal opinion, but you're concerned about their chances of securing the job and how comfortable they will be working in an environment where they may stand out or even be singled out. When people talk about a company 'culture', this is one of the things that matter. Culture refers to 'the way we do things around here' and how you dress is very much part of that.

Also be careful that you don't impose your own standards on your clients. A recruiter I was once working with told me she had a lot of trouble finding suitable temps. When I dug a bit deeper, it turned out that she wanted her temps to be a size eight and to wear Cue suits! After discussing these extremely narrow criteria, she could see that perhaps these standards were not only too high, but that in fact some of her clients would feel uncomfortable having a temp dressed like this when it clashed with their own more relaxed dress code.

At the end of the day, it's not what *you* like that matters, but what your clients like and expect. Your job is to identify their criteria and meet them. If in doubt, it's better for your temp to be overdressed than underdressed on the first day. It's preferable if you have physically been to the company's offices, so you can get a first-hand feel for the culture. Your job is to ensure that the temp fits in and feels comfortable and the client accepts the temp as one of their own team.

3. Booking the temp in for an assignment

It's important to be really specific with assignment details every time you book a temp, but the first time, you need to reiterate some of the 'rules' you mentioned at the interview. Consider the rule that if they are sick, late or need any time off, they are to call you and ask you. To maintain control of the assignment and relationship with your temp and client, all requests, information and approvals need to go through you. Tell the temp that you are there for them. If everything goes through you, you can and will protect them from potentially unpleasant situations where it could be the client's word against theirs. It may be something as simple as asking for a day off.

The temp might ask the client directly and while the client agrees, they resent it and would in fact have said 'no' if you had enquired on the temp's behalf. This can then jeopardise continuation of the assignment or prevent the client from requesting that same temp back. The temp will naturally feel unfairly treated, arguing that the client could have just said 'no', but the reality is that some people, including clients, don't like confrontation and may say 'yes' just to avoid it.

The point is that the whole situation could have been averted if the request had come through you, as you might have already known that the week in question was particularly busy at the client company, so you could have advised your temp that it was unlikely she would get the time off then. Or the client would have simply told you 'no'. Or the client might have said 'yes' if you could organise a replacement – which brings us back to the importance of you having control over the assignment and the hours associated with it. If you have temps taking time off without your knowledge, you miss out on the opportunity to replace them, and the first you will know about it is when you see the time sheet. This makes you look bad to the client as you don't know what your temps are doing, and results in you losing hours and therefore money. The result is that the client receives bad service from you as they were left without a temp for the day. And you weren't even aware!

Also remind your temp of the 'rules' about when and how their time sheet is to be submitted. Remember *specificity is gold*. Be specific about day and exact time. The more specific you are, the less likely things will go wrong, as the instructions are clear and not open to multitudes of interpretations. People can have the right intention but not the same interpretation as you. Eliminate the potential for misunderstandings.

You may want to reiterate rules around mobile phone, Facebook and internet usage. Note that your agency's rules may differ from the client's. If they do, you need to be specific about which rules should be abided by. My view is that the temp works for you and is on-hired to the client company and as such need to abide by your rules rather than the client company's. For instance the client company may say it's okay to use the internet if it's quiet. But your advice is that if it's quiet, ask for more work. Your advice needs to prevail, as 'quiet' is open to interpretation. The client pays for the temp to work, therefore the temp needs to work or at least ask for work. If they can't find any work, perhaps the rule is that the temp calls you. You can then check with the client to verify that there really isn't anything for the temp to do. This avoids any misunderstandings where the client thinks your temp was being lazy on the job. Again you can tell your temp that this covers their back as you are looking out for them.

Apart from the rules, you need to tell the temp exactly what they will be doing on the assignment, who they will be reporting to, hours of work, location of work, duration of assignment, pay rate and who will conduct the work health and safety induction (unless you use a generic online induction system like WorkPro). In addition, it's good temp service to tell them practical information such as where to park, where to get lunch, any company rules and dress code.

4. Regular contact while on assignment

Once in an assignment, you need to be in regular contact with your temp. Remember they work for you and you have an obligation to ensure all is well with them. Remind them that if the client changes their duties, it may entitle them to a higher rate. Ask them to call you weekly at a time that suits them, as if you call them they may be in the middle of something or the boss might be right next to them meaning they can't speak freely. But it can still be good to set a timeframe. For example you might say 'As I will be speaking to the client on a weekly basis, can you please call me by 12pm on Thursdays? That way I can raise any issues you have when I speak to them on Thursday afternoons.' Remember that most people will agree to do something if you tell them how they will benefit from doing it. Simply commanding rarely works, as they can't see the reason for it. Or worse, they may object to being 'bossed' around, which creates the wrong impression of the relationship you want to foster with them.

5. Before the assignment comes to an end

Don't wait until the assignment finishes to start working on the next job for your temp. As you are in weekly contact with your temp and your client, you can and should use these calls to extend the assignment, if both parties are happy. Or if an extension is not possible, you need to tell your temp that you will do everything you can to find them a job to start when this job finishes. Being in control and knowing the timelines will enable you to keep your temps working and prevent them from being booked by other agencies. *Your temps are your assets.* It's very difficult for you to build and grow your hours if you lose your assets. Clients love getting the same temps back as they are more efficient because they already know the ropes of the client company. You cannot offer this service if you lose your temps to other agencies. Worst of all, your competitor may actually offer your temp back to your client! That is heartbreaking and money down the drain.

6. While your temp is out of work

During this period, it's vital that you keep an open line of communication with your temp. They need to know you're looking for work for them and you need to know what they are doing, e.g. if they are actively pursuing other avenues of work. Only speaking to your temps when you have something for them will mean that they are unlikely to be available to do the assignment for you. This differs greatly from how a perm recruiter operates: they will contact the candidate if and when a perm job becomes available. But a temp recruiter *must* find work for their temps and not leave them languishing.

7. Visiting the temp in ongoing assignments

You can also visit your temps as well as speaking to them on a weekly basis. Remember the Boral Masonry story? It's not 'set and forget' when you place a temp. The pay-off for you is the temp feels important and they will also become your best source of information. As they are working on the inside of the client company, they can tell you about projects coming up, resignations, product launches, new system implementations; in short tell you about other opportunities for you to provide services and thereby increase your value to the client, which in turn will deepen your relationship with the client. This information gathering will happen organically as you ask what's happening in the company. Temps will also want to tell you about other temps in the company from your competitors. There may be other decision makers using temps whom you haven't yet made contact with or were not even aware of.

ADDITIONAL IDEAS FOR TEMP CARE

- Temp of the Month or Temp of the Year Awards (these are also a great marketing tool if you get the clients involved in the nominations; I'll cover this in the next chapter on client service)
- temp newsletters
- temp parties; they can be quarterly, semi-annual or annual temp outings, e.g. family picnics, movie nights
- vouchers or other rewards for referring other temps
- birthday cards or gifts
- temp breakfasts or lunches, e.g. monthly
- training sessions; this is great as you get to keep your temps' skill sets up to date
- access to discounts, e.g. to coaches, stylists, home loans, gyms (whatever you can negotiate) for being part of your temp team
- higher pay rate than other agencies

How you want to show your appreciation to your temps is up to you and only limited by your imagination. One thing I know for certain is that the more you do for your temps, the more loyal they will be and the better service you can offer your clients. Another thing about benefits for temps is that word spreads. Back in the 1990s at Ecco, our MD decided that we should pay our temps $1.00 more per hour than other agencies. At first this strategy seemed counter-intuitive as there was high unemployment, which meant that temps were not in a strong position to negotiate a better pay deal. If they didn't want to work at the offered rate, many others would step in instead. However it became clear that this strategy did pay off. Word got out and soon we were being approached by the best temps. Because we had the highest quality temps, we could charge the clients premium rates (it's important that a higher pay rate is borne by the client and not by you, as otherwise it will cut into your hourly margin). When you treat people well, news travels. When you treat them poorly, the news travels even faster, particularly now in the age of Twitter, Facebook and smartphones. Choose not to look after your temps at your peril!

Lastly you can spend a lot of time and money on providing various temp benefits but understand that these are only nice 'extras' to the continuous work you provide them. And if you don't provide them with continuous work, then all these 'extras' are unlikely to work at all. Temps are just like you and me; they have responsibilities and bills to pay. Finding them work is your number-one priority and if you have this mindset, then your desk and hours will flourish.

CHAPTER 11

BEST PRACTICE SERVICE FOR CLIENTS

When a client needs a temp, it may be that they need something done quickly, or it may be a longer-term assignment like a maternity leave position or a special project. Regardless of why they need a temp, it's imperative that you provide *quality, speed and value* in your service delivery.

Being specific and quick will win the assignment nine times out of 10. For me there are some basic but extremely important things that determine how well you provide the temp service, which ultimately determines how successful you're going to be at building a strong and profitable temp desk.

1. Provide a service, not a product

You have to consider whether you provide a 'service' or a 'product' when you supply temps. This is important as you need to be completely clear yourself in order to explain it to the client, when and if required. It will be impossible for you to convince your client if you don't have clarity yourself. My strong conviction is that we provide a 'service', that's to say it's the work we do around finding the right temp and making the match that the clients pay for. They are not paying for the person, as human beings aren't products that we can just pull off the shelf when we need them. If that was the case, then there would be no reason why the client should pay more to one agency than another, as a particular temp may be on both agencies' databases.

Think about when you travel on airlines. A multitude of airlines will get you from A to B. Yet we often choose to travel with a more expensive airline due to the service they provide. You may choose not to travel with a low cost airline because of their poor timeliness record, their poor safety record, their narrower seats, their lack of food or luggage allowance. It may be for one or all of these reasons. It's the same when clients choose which agency they use to hire temps. The deciding factors may be the response time, the ability to secure the same temps again, the comfort of knowing that someone suitable and competent will turn up on the right day. If these and other components of the temp service didn't matter, then everyone would be using a budget, no-frills agency. Yet many clients don't, because they want to deal with an ethical, professional agency, which provides top service and people, while being knowledgeable about and taking care of all compliance issues so the client company is not at risk. If the latter wasn't a huge factor, then more companies would organise their own casuals and temps. But with all the potential risks involved, it's more beneficial for them to outsource this function to an on-hire/temp agency. So ensure that you or someone in your agency has absolute knowledge of compliance issues or knows how to access the information when required.

2. Respond quickly

It follows that if we provide a service, then timeliness becomes important. If you delay in getting back to clients with a firm booking, then you're not providing them with peace of mind. They may not be able to do their jobs properly as they will be wondering at the back of their minds whether they need to give their temp jobs to other agencies, which is detrimental to the client, you and your temps! The client will have to waste more time talking to and dealing with other agencies. You may stand to lose the job and hours. Your temps will lose as you will provide fewer jobs. The speed of response will solely come down to how effective you have been with your interview process, your availability list and your conveying of the rules and working partnership to your temps. Skimping on the process early on will cost you hours in the long run and most likely credibility with temps and clients alike.

If your service doesn't have a set response time (e.g. 20 minutes) you are not delivering best practice service. A set response time is also a way of ensuring the client doesn't go elsewhere. If they don't know when you're going to get back to them and another agency calls them and asks if they have a vacancy, they will most likely say 'yes' as they just want it filled, so they can move on with their own job. If on the other hand, they know you are calling back with a firm booking within 20 minutes, then giving someone else the vacancy would unnecessarily complicate the issue.

3. Be the expert in what you do

If a client places a temp booking with you, you need to advise that you will call them back within 20 minutes with confirmation of the name of the person you've booked for them. If a client asks to interview the temp or see resumes, they are questioning your expertise! Don't agree to this lightly. If you do, it devalues your expertise and they may be treating you like a low cost, no-frills, low expertise recruiter. Once you agree to these terms, you've opened yourself up to time wasters. After all, if the client thinks they have to do your job for you, i.e. look at resumes and interview, then as a logical extension of that thought process they also have a right to reject any or all of your temps. The only occasion I might agree to supplying resumes and interviews for a temp assignment is if it's *the first time* the client deals with me (as they may have had their fingers burnt in the past from dealing with someone less qualified) *and* it's a long-term assignment e.g. maternity leave or long service leave. Otherwise I wish them good luck and ask them to come back if they can't get what they need elsewhere. If a client is worried that the temp might not be up to scratch, then refer them to your temp guarantee. If your company doesn't have a temp guarantee, you need one. If you do the job well, there is virtually *no* risk in providing a guarantee as you simply won't send someone if you don't think they can do the job. Stand up for your expertise!

4. Ask questions

Ask as many questions as you need to to do your job well. (For the types of questions to ask, see 'How to take a quality temp job order'.) Some clients have asked me, the first time I deal with them, if I really need to ask them so many questions. They say that other agencies don't ask that many questions for a temp order. My response is 'I note that you no longer deal with the other agency, so I gather you weren't completely happy with what you were getting?' And, the reason I ask many questions is to ensure that I know all the facts, to enable me to get you the best person for the job. Also the information allows me to properly brief the temp before they arrive, so they are confident and happy as well.'

Sometimes recruiters might feel like they are 'bothering' the clients by asking them questions. If you think that, then I suggest you examine the reason for this feeling, as it's not a thought that's conducive to becoming a true business partner to your clients. Are you feeling at your core that you are behaving like a salesperson and therefore need to get out of the client's way? Or do you think you want to be a true consultant and advisor to the client, but your actions state otherwise? It's a privilege for clients to speak with you, so you can impart your vast business and recruitment knowledge to them – but only if you believe this yourself. Otherwise your behaviour will contradict your intentions and clients will immediately pick up on your ambivalence. So get clear about how you view your role. This also is about standing up for your expertise. If you truly believe you can add value, then don't rush the process of gaining information as this is an opportunity for you to showcase and share your knowledge with your clients. I hear recruiters complain that clients do not value their expertise and won't give them the time of day. The question I have is invariably: 'Do you value your own expertise? And are you behaving accordingly, i.e. are you expecting or even demanding that they give you the time of the day?'

Some recruiters may not like to ask questions as they think they should already know the answers. Well, unless you are a mind reader, there is no way of knowing how each client does what they do. If you don't ask questions or ask too few, you risk getting it wrong. *Specificity is gold*: it allows you to do your job well and avoids potential conflicts.

A TYPICAL CHAIN OF CLIENT INTERACTIONS

Keeping the above doctrine in mind, here is a typical series of interactions with a client during a temp vacancy.

1. The client tells you they need a temp

You take down all the details required for you to have a solid understanding of what they need, who will be looking after the temp, how long the job is for and why they need a temp. The 'why' is crucial as this may open up other opportunities for you to expand your service offering to the client. Maybe they need a temp due to a resignation; then you can ask if you can recruit the perm role for them. Would they consider a temp-to-perm? Is anyone else already recruiting the permanent vacancy for them? This last question is very important as every vacancy has a timeline from when it opens to when it's filled. If you don't ask, you might assume you're at the start of the process, but actually it's been going on for a while. By the time you find someone, the client has already filled the vacancy. When this happens, it's not the client's fault, it's yours! You didn't ask or you weren't *specific* enough with your questions. As mentioned earlier, when something goes wrong, it's usually due to someone not being specific enough. *It's up to you to learn, practice and master specificity.*

Here are some useful questions to ask to determine where in the recruitment timeline you've come in and also if the client is agreeable to leaving the job with you exclusively:

- What is the reason for this vacancy?
- How long has the job been vacant?
- What steps have you taken to date to fill this position?
- Have you listed the position with any other agencies?

If not listed elsewhere:

- I'm more than happy to work on this position for you. I'm confident we can get a good temp for you. I will pull out all stops to do so. What we find works best, is if you can leave the vacancy with us exclusively for 20 minutes. That way you get the best available temp we have and you can relax and have complete peace of mind that we will fill the job for you. If for some reason, we can't fill it in the 20 minutes, we will let you know as well.

If already listed elsewhere:

- How many agencies are working on it?
- May I ask why the position is still vacant?

If not happy with the temps they've been sent so far:

- If you haven't been happy with the temps put forward to you so far; what hasn't been right?
- I can work on it and feel certain that I can fill it for you, but will need you to give it to me exclusively as my job is also to work on behalf of our temps, and I need to know that this is a legitimate job that they can secure when I offer it to them. Can you do that?

2. Call the client back within the time promised

Once you have all the job details, repeat them back to the client for verification, then tell them you're going to call them back in 20 minutes. Agree on what the current time is first!

When you call back, give them the name of the booked temp and confirm the hourly rate verbally. Then email the client with the rate and ask them to authorise it. If it's the first time you've dealt with them, also send them your terms and conditions for authorisation.

3. If you can't find a suitable temp

If you haven't been able to find a temp in the given time, tell the client clearly what you will do, e.g., you have two people in mind, who are both at work and you won't be able to speak to them until their lunch hour, so if the client is agreeable, you will call the client back by 1pm (not 'this afternoon'). Always be *specific* with times and actions, so they know exactly what to expect. That way, you are setting the expectation levels, which you can and will meet. If you don't, the clients will make up their own expectations and you may disappoint them without even knowing what they were expecting or wanting!

Call back by the agreed time and confirm the booking, or if you still don't have anyone and you're unsure whether you can fill the job, bite the bullet and tell the client to go elsewhere as well. While this is not an ideal situation, it is far preferable to leaving the client in the lurch, i.e. with no temp and no time for any other recruiters to find someone. To me, that's an absolute cardinal sin. And for the record, I have never lost a client by not being able to fill a temp job on a particular day and sending them elsewhere. They would always come back and often comment on how the service and temp they ended up with from another agency weren't very good.

4. First day 15-minute check

On the first day of the assignment, I call 15 minutes after the temp's expected arrival time and speak to the client: 'I'm calling to check that Mary has arrived safely with you?' If the client is busy showing the temp around, the receptionist can often confirm for you if the temp is there. Tell the client or the receptionist that you will be calling back in four hours to do the four-hour check.

5. First day 4-hour check

If the temp started at 9am, then call at 1pm, if the temp started at 8.30am, then call at 12.30pm: 'I'm calling to check that Mary has settled in and that you're happy with how everything is going?' The client will usually express delight or say that they've been too busy to check. It doesn't matter either way, as you have it on record that you did the four-hour check. The reason I do this check is related to the temp guarantee I work under. The conditions of the guarantee are that if the client is not happy after the first four hours, then she doesn't have to pay for that temp and also gets a replacement temp for free for the next seven hours. As it's service the client pays for, it's up to us to make that four-hour call rather than wait for them to call us to say the temp isn't working out. It's not that we expect there to be trouble; on the contrary, it's another opportunity to showcase our commitment to best practice customer service to the client. Also, in the unlikely event that the temp is going to be finished up, then you don't want to prolong the day as the temp is still entitled to get paid.

6. Weekly checks

If the assignment is ongoing, then you need to be doing a weekly check with your client. I tell the client upfront that I'll be doing the weekly checks to ensure their continued satisfaction with the temp. Occasionally a temp may start to feel so comfortable that they start to take liberties with the client company, e.g. taking time off or not doing certain tasks, so one way of keeping on top of this is to check in on a weekly basis. As your temp is calling you weekly, you can also facilitate any feedback both ways between temp and client. I prefer to speak to the temp first, so I can give the client any feedback and also resolve any potential queries for the temp. It doesn't have to be a long call; it's more about providing an open line of communication in case it is needed.

Of course, this is also a good time to ask the client: 'What else can I assist you with for next week?' Every call is a potential business development call, if you *ask* for work. For time poor recruiters, it's good time management to ask the question while you have your client on the phone. That way you don't have to make separate service calls and business development calls. You can also ask on these weekly service calls: 'Who else hires temps in your company?' or 'Who else might benefit from our services?' Toward the end of the assignment, you can ask the client if the temp is still finishing on the originally booked finish date. If they are uncertain, offer to call them the day before the assignment is due to finish, so you know if it's time for you to work on getting the temp their next assignment. I will ask on a Thursday if the temp is still finishing on the Friday. If the client is uncertain, I will tell him that I'll call again on the Friday morning as I don't want to leave the temp stranded and out of work. Sometimes the client will extend the temp rather than risk losing them if there's a possibility they may still be required. However if they are finishing up, you can ask the client, after establishing that they were happy with the temp: 'Who else might be able to use Mary's services?' You'll be surprised how helpful clients are when they really like the temp. You're asking them for a referral for Mary rather than for yourself in this instance.

7. On-site visits

It's always advantageous to visit clients if they use recruitment services as they will tell you far more face-to-face than over the phone or on email. If you have temps with a client, you can schedule regular visits depending on the volume of temps used and whether the client's location is convenient to you. Clients may tell you they don't have a need, but when you turn up they are just as likely to give you a vacancy because of the convenience of being able to do it on the spot. The rewards for visiting clients are well worth it.

If you ask your clients to nominate for 'Temp of the Month', you can also choose to give the award to a temp they have nominated who is still on site. I call the client and tell them that their nominated temp will be getting the 'Temp of the Month' award for that month, and at a time that suits them, I'd like to come out to do the presentation and take some photos. The prize doesn't have to be extravagant; it might be a double Gold Class movie pass, $100 David Jones card or a bunch of flowers. What *is* important is that they receive a certificate for their resume folder and that you make a *big* deal out of the presentation. With your client's involvement, you will set up both the temp and the client for photos, which you can put into the temp newsletter. It's a double 'win', as your temp feels valued and appreciated, and your client feels listened to as it was their nomination that lead to the award. You also have high visibility within the client company to other internal hirers and possibly temps from other agencies who are left wondering why their agency isn't visiting them with gifts and certificates.

ADDITIONAL WAYS TO ADD EXTRA SERVICE AND VALUE TO CLIENTS

- Offer online time sheets for them to verify rather than having to print time sheets each week.
- Offer bulk time sheets for multiple temps, so they don't have to verify several individual time sheets, but rather can sign off all the temps on the one sheet.
- Offer to go through their on-site work health and safety induction yourself, so you can then conduct the on-site induction for all future temps, meaning they don't have to supply a staff member to do it every single time you have a new temp starting.
- Offer them a 24-hour phone number, so they can call you out of hours if they need a temp. That way there won't be any downtime while they wait for your office opening hours. With the client's approval, give your 24-hour number to their receptionist or call-centre manager as well, who can then call you directly if they know they or others can't come to work.
- Offer to benchmark test the client's staff to identify any internal skills gaps which could be 'plugged' by your temps. This can be done with a number of proprietary tools and charged on a cost-recovery basis or at a markup.
- Offer to manage all the temps, not just from your agency, but also temps from other agencies. Many agencies are poor at temp management, and technically it is the client's responsibility. But if the client agrees, this means all the temps need to go through *you* for time off, lateness or illness, which means *you* get to replace the temps who can't work, whether from your agency or not.
- Keep them updated on changes in compliance and legislation, e.g. in work health and safety, award increases and workplace conditions.
- Keep them updated on industry-specific news or general business knowledge.

HOW TO TAKE A QUALITY TEMP JOB ORDER

A good temp job order means you know *exactly* what the temp will be doing, who they report to, their standard hours of work, the duration of the assignment, the reason for the vacancy and any other relevant info. When clients ask for a temp, they will often ask for a position title, e.g. 'Send me a PA', but we all know that no two personal assistant jobs are the same.

So ask questions about the following:

Duties: What do you want the temp to do? What percentage of their day will be spent doing that? What software will they be using? If the client isn't forthcoming or they don't know the answers to your questions, ask if you can speak to the PA that's currently in the job.

Reporting: Who is the temp to report to (name and title)? Will they work for other people as well? Who has priority? If there are clashing priorities, who will they check with to see what should be done first?

Hours of work: e.g. 9am to 5pm with half an hour for lunch (temps aren't paid for their lunch break). Ask if there is a set time the temp goes to lunch. If the company has flexi-time, you need to ask if it's better that the temp has set hours to suit the person(s) they are going to work for. This is easier for you as the consultant to control.

Duration of the assignment: Clients need to be specific about this. If not, you need to impress upon them how important it is. They may say 'indefinite' or 'ongoing', which may mean three months or six months. We have no idea of what they have in mind. It's not good service to the temp if we can't tell them, and if we don't tell them, it ends up not being good service to the client. We might say to the temp it's for three months when the client really wants 12 months. After three months the temp may want to leave, which means more work for you as a consultant as you have to refill and bad service for the client as they have to retrain. One way of getting the clients to be specific is to counter with something outrageous and exaggerated, e.g. when they say it's ongoing, you can ask 'will it be for two years then?' The client will say 'Oh no, not that long, probably more like four months.' Then you have the information you need. Another scenario is the client may not want to tell you upfront that it's for four months as they want to see if they like the temp first. It's helpful to say: 'If it may be longer term, it's important that you let me know, so I can ensure that the person I send you is actually available for the whole duration. As they work as temps, you can finish them up any time, so if for some reason you no longer need their services, then all you need to do is let me know and I'll take care of it for you.'

Reason for the vacancy: Illness, maternity, long service, project work, resignation: there are many possibilities. The reason they give you can telegraph other opportunities for you, e.g. a perm vacancy or long-term contract or temp job. Therefore it's imperative that you ask the question and wait for the answer. Don't ask and then give them options like: 'So what's the reason for this temp vacancy? Is it because of overload?' First of all it shows a lack of respect for the client if you ask and tell them the answer. Secondly you won't find out as much as if you simply wait for the answer. If it is due to a resignation, make sure you ask if they will take a temp-to-perm. Then you can approach your perm candidate base as well as your temps who want a perm job. You will know which of your temp and perm pools to go to.

Any other relevant info: For PAs, for example, do they need to buy personal gifts or do other out-of-the-ordinary things? In one case I know of, an Asian company's CEO had to have a plate with eight biscuits laid out every day as the number eight is lucky and invites prosperity. He never actually ate the eight biscuits, but it was a vital part of the PA's duties. Other duties may include going to the post office to pick up the mail; for this and other errands, ask whether the temp uses their own car and receives a car allowance or if they use a company car. If it's a company car, does that mean the temp must have a full licence for insurance purposes rather than a restricted provisional licence?

You can see from the above examples that you need to dig deep into what the temp job is about, so that you can a) tell the temp what they will be doing so they are confident, b) be confident yourself that you've chosen the best temp for that specific assignment, c) offer the client the best service by making the best match in terms of skills, availability and culture fit.

Regarding the example of the PA laying out the biscuits, be aware that not all PAs are willing to do this sort of thing as they consider it to be beneath them. If you don't know this is a daily duty, you could inadvertently put a person in who refuses to do this and thus cause trouble. Particularly if the temp is to work for the CEO, the consequence may be that you don't even get to replace that temp as the CEO may see you as incompetent! Then you've lost not only the hours, but also your professional credibility, which could have been avoided by you asking specific questions. Believe me, the more specific you are at the job-order-taking stage, the easier it is for you to shine and grow your hours. Don't be afraid to ask. If need be, simply explain why you need to know. Remember this is your area of expertise, so the onus is on you to ask, not on the client to tell you!

CHAPTER 12

QUALITY CONTROL

Providing an outlet for clients to give you feedback is a must, as any feedback is an opportunity to deepen the relationship you have. You may have had a bad experience with a service provider yourself and decided not to return as a customer. You will probably have told at least one other person about it, so your negative experience has the potential to impact someone else's future buying decision. And in the age of social media, you may have posted your decision not to go back to your 500 friends on Facebook. Or tweeted your experience to your 389 followers on Twitter or maybe even both. Recently a mum posted that a certain supermarket brand of nappies was dangerous as her toddler had parts of the nappy down her throat. This story made front page news and shortly after, the supermarket in question recalled all nappies of that particular brand. A client's negative experience with your company may not elicit that level of interest, but we know that brand damage is very real and difficult to bounce back from.

On the other hand, if a client loves your service, you'd probably like to know about it as well. With their permission you may be able to use their positive feedback as a testimonial to enhance your sales process.

Either way you need to create a feedback loop that's easy for the clients to use *and* for you to respond. If it's negative feedback, respond *immediately* as there's nothing worse than taking the time to give feedback and not hearing anything more about it.

I used to own a car made by a French car manufacturer. While I loved this car, I didn't love that it would stall every 8000 kilometres and that I had to be towed each time. Every year this company would ask me for feedback in a satisfaction survey. Twice I described in great detail what seemed to be wrong with the car. No one ever responded, leaving me frustrated and disappointed. So only embark on this route if you are serious and committed to getting feedback, responding to the client and preferably fixing the problem.

Being committed in itself is not enough, as you also need a rigorous process in place to back up this commitment. Recently a friend of mine bought a phone case from a well-known phone manufacturer. She asked the salesperson for a case that would fit the latest model phone, which her son had purchased. When she brought the case home, it didn't fit. She subsequently complained in the online survey form and promptly received a phone call from their customer service department. Unfortunately they rang at an inconvenient time. They asked her when they should call back, but failed to do so at the nominated time. This company gets brownie points for asking for feedback and then responding to the feedback, but unfortunately doesn't seem to have a process that guarantees that the follow-up call happens. For your temp desk, decide what your feedback process is going to be, so your quality control can continuously evolve in line with your own standards and client expectations.

Some recruitment companies have a particular person that looks after this area, e.g. a client experience manager. If you don't have the overheads or the volume of business to have a dedicated person for this role, that's okay, as long as the feedback request loop begins and ends with someone other than the consultant who does the actual recruiting and liaising with the client. The reason for this is that while the client may want something in the service delivery to be tweaked, they may really like the consultant and not want to upset the relationship they have with that person. In my opinion it's better if the client can clearly see that their feedback goes to the general manager or managing director of the agency. It allows them to be open about the service delivery process. I've had instances where clients have loved the service provided, but, for example, didn't like the layout of our invoices. As this kind of thing is nothing to do with the temp consultant, it makes sense that there is a forum for the client to bring this up.

Feedback can be requested via an emailed feedback form generated from an administrator's email address but sent on behalf of the director. If the feedback form is posted as a hard copy, then make sure you attach a reply-paid self-addressed envelope addressed to the MD.

A good feedback form for temps needs to measure client satisfaction in two separate areas:

The quality of the temp: their skill level, the client's willingness to reemploy the same temp and whether they would nominate this temp for the Temp of the Month award.

The quality of the consultant's service: response time, how accurately they matched the temp to their requirements, maybe even whether they would recommend this temp consultant for a Consultant of the Year award (if you have such an award).

Don't make the feedback too onerous or people won't take the time to do it. If a form takes more than a few minutes to fill out, it makes me wonder whether the writer could have spent more time working on the quality of their questions to condense them into exactly what they want to know. Too many questions reveals a lack of clarity on the part of the questioner as to what they consider to be important. At the other end of the spectrum is the use of the Net Promoter Score, which asks just one question: 'How likely are you to recommend our company/product/service to your friends and colleagues?' The clients are asked to answer using a scale from 1-10. The score is then used to engage customers in a conversation about why they gave the score they did. So it's a tool to engage customers, which also provides the opportunity to further the discussion and turn their perception around if the score was low.

For you to embed a feedback process for quality control purposes, you need to first get clear on what it is you want to measure, what you're going to do with the information collected and who is going to do it. Feedback is your friend; get it, value it and act on it!

CHAPTER 13

SEVEN WAYS TO SUPERCHARGE YOUR TEMP HOURS

There are many, many things you can do to grow your desk. The secret is to do them *confidently, competently* and most importantly *consistently*. Going back to the airline example: it's no good to deliver sensational service on some flights and not on others. Consistency is almost enough to build a brand on. Have you ever heard people say they like to go to McDonalds because regardless of where the store is in the world, you know exactly what you're going to get? That brand consistency is in itself worth millions of dollars.

To grow your temp desk, you need to have consistent processes that your clients become familiar with and come to rely on for the smooth running of their businesses. Being known for consistent service quality is better than being so generic that you can't stand out in a crowd. The recruitment market is notoriously crowded due to the low entry barrier. According to recent figures supplied by the Recruitment and Consulting Services Association, there are approximately 4,000 agencies in Australia and 17,000 in the USA.

Keeping this in mind, here are some processes you can implement and execute brilliantly to stand out:

1. Marketing the same temps back

Always record a client's satisfaction with each particular temp. So if your temp is called Susie, ask if they would have Susie back if there's a requirement in future. *Every* time Susie is available or due to finish an assignment, you phone all the clients that Susie has worked for and ask them if they need Susie before you book her elsewhere. The conversation may sound like this: 'Hi Bob, remember Susie who worked for you a couple of months ago in accounts? She's just become available and I know how much you liked having her on your team when Janice was away, so I'm calling to give you first dibs on her before I book her elsewhere. She really enjoyed working with you as well. What work might you have that Susie can do? As Susie is such a good temp, it's my job to keep her in work and happy, so if you're not sure whether you have something for her, then I'll be calling other clients to secure her some work. Would you like me to check back with you later today?'

Let me ask you: have you ever been in a situation where another agency has sent 'your' temp back to 'your' client? It hurts right? So make sure you are on top of your temps' availabilities at all times. From a service point of view, it's excellent service to both your temp and your client. And so easy to do!

2. Becoming an expert in your client's peak periods

Every business, government department or industry has its own peak periods. Providing first class service means knowing and anticipating what your clients might need and then offering them that requirement. When you think back to first-class service you've received, isn't it often when you've been offered something over and above what you expected or before you even thought about it that impressed you? Last year I was holidaying in Thailand with my family and on Christmas Eve there was a present for my son on his hotel room pillow when we returned from dinner. It's the little things that make all the difference, like having your car washed when it's in for a service. Something extra that they thought about, that makes you feel they care. This is what most people consider to be exceptional service.

When I worked with a few electronics companies, I quickly learnt that their peak period to cope with the increased consumer demand for electronics products at Christmas was all over by the end of September. Their ramp-up period was early as the products had to be ordered, stocked and distributed in the months before Christmas. Not weeks or days, when we the consumers are thinking about Christmas. This led me to talk to them about their upcoming temp needs in June or July; just as they were about to plan for the busy period. Your aim is to be part of your clients' normal planning and execution process, not an afterthought. This is your way of showing you understand their challenges and that you care!

3. Using *every* reference check to market temps back

As discussed in chapter 6, at the end of a normal reference check you should always take the opportunity to try to place the temp with that company again. The only deviation from this rule is if the referee doesn't recommend the person you're reference checking or they've already said they wouldn't have them back. Do this thoroughly as you get to display your expertise here by the questions you ask. I have had referees ask if I am always this thorough when reference checking, to which I reply 'It's my job to be thorough. As employers, we have to be able to use and rely on each other's experiences with any given employee as a means of predicting their future performance.' This is also an organic segue to asking right at the end: 'It would be remiss of me not to ask if you're the person who hires temps in your company?' If they are and they've said they'd be happy to have that temp back, then you ask: 'Well, Susie is actually available for work from next Monday and she did express interest in working with you again. Would you like me to book her for you?' If they are not the person who is the decision maker or person who hires, then ask for the name of that person. When you phone that person, you now have a 'warm' link: 'Jack in accounts mentioned that you're the person to speak to regarding the hiring of temporary staff. Is this a convenient time for us to have a chat about how you go about doing that?'

4. Adhering to your best practice service

In chapter 11, I spoke about the necessity of making weekly service calls to your clients when you have temps working with them. The purpose of these calls is to ensure that your client is happy with the work the temp is doing, to facilitate any communication between the temp and client, to check on the temp's finishing date so you don't lose sight and your temp gets booked by another agency, *and* to ask what else you can help them with. When you call regularly with the same agenda, the clients get used to what you're calling about and will in fact mentally prepare for your questions. Clients have said to me that they knew I'd be asking if anyone else could use the temp, so they'd already made enquiries on my behalf. Training your clients to work for you is great!

5. Asking the 'magical' sales questions

When I was a young rookie recruiter, my boss Nigel Harse (who figures in chapter 16) taught us to ask one of the following questions on every call to clients:

a) 'Who else might be able to use this temp?' (Asking for a referral for the temp, which clients are happy to give if they are happy with the temp)
b) 'Who else do you know who might be able to use my services?' (Asking for a referral for you, which they are happy to give if your service is good)
c) 'What else can I help you with?'

Nigel was a tough boss; he would make consultants call the client back if they had hung up without asking one of the above questions! That would be so embarrassing that the consultants never forgot again (at least not when he was within earshot).

I call them 'magical' sales questions because they really work. Most consultants might ask: 'Is there anything else I can help you with?', to which the answer is more often than not a 'no'. The intent of this question is clearly to elicit more business, but the problem is that it's a closed question and too narrow. Usually in sales, we learn to ask closed questions when we want to close, i.e. make a sale. Here we first need to uncover any additional needs, so the open magical sales questions will do just that. *Then* we can close when we know what to sell.

Also the beauty of the three questions is that they are suitably broad. I once asked question b) and the client said: 'I'm pretty sure that no-one else is hiring in our company at the moment, but I had a beer with a mate last Thursday who mentioned he's hiring an accounts person.' Naturally I asked for the friend's details so I could call and get the job, which I did. The friend was very responsive and was happy to be offered the help from his friend and myself.

Another time I asked question c) on a Friday evening of one of my key accounts whom I had dealt with for years. He said: 'Well I do need a permanent staff member, but you only deal with temps.' This wasn't a particularly proud moment for me as I realised I obviously hadn't been reminding him enough of our other services. I immediately said that while I didn't personally look after permanent recruitment, I had two excellent perm recruiters in my team whose perm service equalled what he was used to on the temporary side. Fortunately I was able to uncover and secure the permanent job order for our business.

Has it ever happened to you that you deal with a client for temps, but then they give a permanent job order to another agency and you wonder why? Well clients can get used to you wearing a certain hat, and maybe you weren't disciplined enough or consistent enough in asking the magical sales questions.

6. Adhering to your sales cycle

As this is a book about the process of building and growing a temp desk rather than a book about sales, I haven't yet touched on the necessity of having a sales cycle, other than when I mentioned that we need on average between four and seven touch points to convert a prospect to a client. A sales cycle is a process whereby we ensure that every prospect *and* client is contacted on a regular basis, so they feel you care enough to call them when they don't have any vacancies for you. If you don't have such a process that you can follow consistently, then you're still working the transactional recruitment model, which clients are increasingly turning away from and some are even quite offput by.

The challenges for most recruiters in having a sales cycle are twofold:

Setting up a meaningful call cycle: Some people call every client with the same frequency without regard to their actual potential usage. So the client who uses five temps a week is called with the same regularity as the client who uses one temp every six months. It makes more sense for you and the client to schedule the calls in line with a client's temp usage.

Prioritising the time to follow it: What tends to happen is that when a recruiter has lots of jobs to fill they neglect keeping in touch with clients. Then when all their jobs are filled or they are short on their KPIs, that's when they get on the phone, with desperation in their hearts that then leaks into their conversations. Make no mistake; clients can tell when you're desperate, when you're calling in the hope of making a quick sale, when you're really on the phone for yourself rather than for them. It shows in the language you use, in your lack of regard for their needs and probably in your preparation for the call. In addition, you need to be working on a continuous pipeline of job orders, not just seeking them when you run out of jobs, as it's already too late then for the current week, month or maybe even the quarter!

7. Successfully juggling your three critical tasks every day

You may recall from chapter 1 that great temp consultants make sure they do their three critical tasks every day:

Finding quality temps: source, attract, secure and retain great temps with the desired skill sets.

Finding quality jobs for your temps: contacting clients by phone, in person or via email.

Matching the right temps to the right clients: regardless of whether that particular client has a job vacancy or not, offering the client someone who you know would suit their business especially if their skill set is hard to find.

You may regard doing the three critical tasks as a time-management challenge, but as everyone has exactly the same amount of hours in a day, isn't it interesting how some people seem to get more done? They may be working hard, but then I'm sure so are you. The difference is that successful people ensure they do the important things first. And the three critical tasks aren't just important, but critical if you want to succeed as a top-tier temp consultant. Think of it as critical task management rather than time management. Thinking about it this way changed the perspective for quite a few of my coaching clients. Sure, you may have some reluctance and therefore put off making client calls, but think of Brian Tracy's book on procrastinating, *Eat that Frog* (Berrett-Koehler Publishers, 2006), which advises that you tackle the hardest task first so that the rest of the day is easier. And every call is more practice. Remember that mastery comes with 10,000 hours of doing the same task. Start *now*, so you can reach mastery sooner.

Even if you only call two clients today, remember how many avenues you have of marketing your temp services: reference checks and service calls as well as your sales cycle. Think broadly and do everything as an organic whole rather than thinking: 'now I must do marketing'. If done correctly then everything you do is marketing to clients or temps.

CHAPTER 14

BECOME AN EXPERT TO ADD VALUE

Regardless of what type of recruitment you do, you will potentially be working with two levels of branding. At the macro level, the agency you work for (or own) will have a brand that is known for something. It might be known for RPO (recruitment process outsourcing), permanent recruitment, headhunting or temporary recruitment and management. At the micro level is your personal brand. Let me give you some examples of these two levels:

Macro level: A coaching client of mine in Melbourne specialises in providing receptionists, which may seem like a very narrow niche, but as this is their speciality they have become extremely good at it. They don't try to be everything to everybody. But they can provide receptionists to any type and size of company.

Micro level: While working at Ecco Personnel, I chose to focus on the awards and industrial relations area to hone my knowledge. I had a natural interest in this topic, but it was both useful and necessary for me to grow temp desks, branches and staff. Because I focused on learning everything I could in this area, I had the information at my fingertips or knew how to access information when required (this was in the pre-internet days). This led to me becoming known as the 'awards person'. My colleagues would tell their clients that I could help them with any award info they required.

Years ago a client of mine who was a CFO would bounce tricky recruitment-related questions off me. For example, she would ask about unfair dismissal laws and how she needed to go about giving warnings. In these types of conversations, I would *always* start with a disclaimer, and go on to give my opinion: 'I'm not a lawyer, so you should check with your lawyer to be certain. However *my* understanding is that you can only give a warning about one specific issue at a time. Then you must allow enough time for the employee to demonstrate that they understand and improve before you move on to another specific issue.' The CFO found these conversations helpful as she didn't have anyone she could talk about this with in her company because of the confidential nature of the matter and due to her position in the company. While I offered this advice free of charge, it benefited me by deepening the relationship I had with her and it also meant that I was privy to staff movements prior to them occurring. There's a lot of talk in recruitment about being a trusted advisor, and one way to do this is to build your expertise and offer a consulting advisory service as a value-add to your recruitment service. Occasionally I hear recruiters complain that their clients don't know something which they consider to be basic knowledge. My response is why should your clients know your area of expertise? If they did, they wouldn't need you! Your job is to educate them, which also allows you to put on the trusted advisor hat and demonstrate your expertise and professionalism.

Another 'brand' I developed, albeit organically rather than strategically, was becoming known as the 'electronics' expert. By dealing with the two largest electronics companies in the country, I automatically attracted electronics staff and people who had a particular interest in working in the electronics industry, and thereby became far more valuable to my electronics clients, as well as being attractive to other electronics companies who became my clients.

This is why I always recommend approaching your clients' competitors. You already have industry knowledge, understand their lingo and most likely have temps with industry experience, which will save your clients time, money and effort when hiring temps from you.

So when thinking about how you can become an 'expert' or known for something; think on both the macro and micro levels.

On the macro or company level, you may not be able to influence a lot, but you could choose to work a niche within a niche: what is known as a vertical market. An example of a vertical market would be financial planners in the finance industry. Recruitment business owners will, in my experience, listen to a sales strategy that will benefit them and the bottom line. For example, your agency may specialise in accounting shared services and you choose to focus on the banking sector or the manufacturing sector. While you could say that accounting shared services are very similar regardless of the type of company, there are still nuances that will make you an 'expert'.

Expertise can be in an array of areas:

- Industry expertise, e.g. electronics.
- Service specific expertise, e.g. RPO (recruitment process outsourcing).
- Recruitment expertise, e.g. setting up and running assessment centres. I set up and ran assessment centres for Goodman Fielder's shared services accounts department. This meant that *all* applicants to this area of Goodman Fielder had to come through us to work there. It also meant that if I saw someone who I knew would be the right fit for the company, I could usually get them in as a temp until they could attend the next assessment centre, which we only ran approximately every eight weeks depending on need. As I had become an expert in what Goodman Fielder needed, I could persuade the managers that hiring the person as a temp would 'keep them off the streets' so we didn't risk losing them to another employer.
- Specific temporary service expertise, e.g. rostering and managing large temp numbers like retail, hospitality or blue collar staff.
- Systems specific expertise, e.g. SAP.
- Your client's specific needs expertise, e.g. I had clients who confided in me about staff who were in critical roles and were likely to call in sick, so I would already have a replacement on standby, and I knew which

departments would have the most sick days, so I prearranged for some temps to be trained in their systems ready to be booked. This also meant that it was difficult for other agencies to get their temps in, as the client had trained my temps, so they had 'skin in the game'. It was in their interests to use the temps that they had invested time and money in training.

These ideas and others can work on the company level while there is still plenty of scope for you to develop your own area of expertise and brand. All it takes is imagination or inspiration to decide what you want to specialise in and then the hard work of acquiring and maintaining that expertise begins.

CHAPTER 15

ESSENTIAL TEMP METRICS

Have you ever heard the question: 'How do you eat an elephant?' The answer is: 'One bite at a time'. Pretty obvious when you think about it, as we can tend to be overwhelmed by tasks when they seem big and insurmountable. There is a similar Chinese proverb that says: 'Every thousand-mile journey starts with a single step'.

Growing a temp desk is the same, you just need to know what your bites or steps are. For example, if you're running a white-collar temp desk, then your *ultimate* aim in my view is to bill 1000 hours per week (per consultant). This equates to having 30 temps out per week as the average week worked per temp is approximately 33 hours. This average allows for part-timers and people having time off. If you currently have 10 temps out with approximately 330 hours, then your goal *this week* might be to keep the 10 temps out and add another two temps.

If I was working with you to grow your desk, I would expect you to know every morning: how many temps you've got out that day, how many hours you have for that week and how many temp job orders you still need to get for that week (based on your average number of hours worked per temp) to reach your weekly goal towards building your desk. Some recruiters say they don't know what the hours are until they get the time sheets in from the temps, but this is a weak excuse for not being in control of their desk! Imagine if you worked in an office and had people reporting to you. Would you be expected to know who was in and who was away at any given time? Well running a temp desk is no different; the expectation I have of you is the same. The *big* difference is you have to be on top of your temp and client conversations in order to know what's happening, as you're working as a remote manager with your workforce spread between different sites and sometimes even different states or countries. As you're not in the same office as your temps, you can't physically see who is in, but you still need to know.

Here are the reasons why temps must call you when they are sick or away: you know what's going on; you can offer your client a replacement for the duration of absence; temps are less likely to take time off if they don't really need to; and you will know exactly how many temps you need to have out each day to reach your weekly hours goal. If you wait for the time sheets to come in, then all you can do is establish that you didn't make your target, as it's after the week has finished. But if you know where you stand every single day, then that means you can make a concerted effort to reach your shortfall every hour of your week. This is the difference between being proactive and reactive. The best and most successful consultants understand that being proactive means ensuring the three critical tasks are done every day regardless of how many emails they might have in their inbox.

RECORDING YOUR METRICS

Here are the figures you need to record for each week and adjust daily as you get more information (e.g. people calling in sick or new job orders).

Number of hours: This is the *only* true measure of your income if you bill by the hour. You could have 100 temps out, but if they only did a three-hour shift each that week, then you would bill 300 hours and have done a *lot* of work for very little return, as each temp has to be booked, rostered and confirmed. If you deal with contractors and bill by the day, then change this metric to number of days booked per week.

Number of temps out: This is important as you can tell from how much this figure fluctuates daily and weekly whether you have a solid group of long-term temps out or if they are mostly short-term assignments.

Number of clients: If you have temps out with multiple hirers in a company, then count them as separate clients. In a company with decentralised temp recruitment, you will be able to determine how may hirers there are, and this will enable you to gauge your coverage, rather than assuming you have *all* the business.

Also the number of clients tells you at a glance whether you're putting all your eggs in one basket. A recruitment company once had all their temps with one company that owned a petrol station chain. The relationship was very solid, but through no fault of theirs, the agency lost all their business overnight as the client closed all the stores and moved interstate.

For this reason, you need to have a mix of clients with no more than 80% of your business coming from 20% of your clients. Having 100% of your temp business with one client is suicide for a temp desk and potentially for the agency! The 80/20 rule also ensures that you have a mix of different-sized clients in your portfolio. If you only deal with small companies, it will take you a lot more work to get to the 1000 hours. If you only deal with large companies, you may get to 1000 hours quicker, but you also have a lot more at stake. The safe and sustainable strategy is to have a mix of client companies ranging across small, medium and large companies.

Number of job orders taken: All job orders taken that week, updated daily, so that they can be compared with job orders filled.

Number of job orders filled: This is a good measure of how extensive your temp pool is and how well you can 'control' the temps. By 'control' I mean whether you have good enough rapport with your temps to get their commitment quickly, or whether you spend all your time chasing them only for them to say they can't do the assignment for you. If your aim is to provide best practice service with a 20-minute call back service, then the number of jobs filled per week should equal the number of jobs taken.

Number of advance job orders: These are job orders in hand to start after the current week. These are like gold (if filled) as the more advance job orders you get, the better organised you can be with your temp pool and also you will know how many hours you've already got in the weeks ahead. This is your temp hours pipeline.

Number of lost job orders: These need to be recorded so you can identify *why* they were lost:

- Was it a noncore business job you decided to take on but then couldn't fill? For example, you might specialise in office support, but the client asked you to find a mechanic and you readily agreed without thinking the consequences through.
- Do you need to recruit more temps with the skill set that was required for the job?
- Was it a client who was wasting your time? Did you allow this to happen due to not being *specific* enough with the job order timeline, the exclusivity or the 'rules'?
- Do you need to get better at negotiations? Did the client force you into a 'dollars and cents' conversation when you should have been having a 'value' conversation?
- Was it lost due to lack of temp control, i.e. did the temp refuse to do this assignment for you?

If you understand the reasons, you can learn from them. In coaching, there is *no* failure, only feedback. The only 'failure' would be if you didn't learn from the feedback in any given situation. This is how we improve and get closer to mastery.

Number of temps interviewed: Attracting temps to work for you is one of your critical tasks, so this needs to measured. Measure how many people you interview, how many you take onto your books and where they come from (referrals, Seek, networking, etc). That way when you need someone with a particular skill set, you can go straight to the source where the best temps with those skills came from last time.

Number of phone calls made to clients: These are marketing phone calls and as they are part of your three critical tasks, these need to happen daily. You can only count these if you ask for work and you speak to decision makers. If you count all calls, then this will make your calls to job orders ratio blow out. For example you might make 20 marketing calls per week and get five job orders; that gives you a ratio of four calls to one job order, which is excellent. But if you count all calls, even non-marketing ones, you might not get any job orders with 20 calls, and then the temptation is to think that you need to make more calls, whereas in fact your calls just aren't targeted enough.

Number of client visits: Again these need to be with the decision makers. It's *not* a client visit if you drop your business card to the receptionist and ask for the hiring contact's name. As with phone calls, you need to measure only activity with a decision maker and you can only count the visit if you proactively ask for business. If you arrive and give your clients some Easter eggs and wish them happy Easter; that is *not* a client visit in the real sense as you haven't asked for any job orders.

Number of finishers: This is important to measure as you may have 30 people out this week, but if you have 25 people finishing this week, then you know you will have to work *very* hard to find 25 job orders for the following week just to maintain the same numbers.

Number of new starters: If you have 25 finishers but 26 new starters for the following week, you are right on track as you've managed to add one extra temp. When you do your weekly projections, you can use this formula:

> Hours in hand = All temps continuing in their assignments - All finishers this week + All new starters next week.

Then you can look at your hours target for that week and work out how many more job orders you need based on your average number of hours worked per temp.

If you measure all the above information on a daily basis each week for a period of 12 weeks, I can tell at a glance where you need strengthening through training or mentoring.

I can see this by working out the following ratios:

Hours to temps = Average hours worked per temp e.g. 657 hours: 22 temps = 29.86 average hours worked per temp

Temps to clients = Average number of temps working for each client e.g. 22 temps: 5 clients = 4.4 temps per client

Calls to visits = Average number of marketing calls per visit e.g. 55 calls: 3 visits = 28.33 calls per visit

Calls to job orders = Average number of marketing calls made to get each job order e.g. 55 calls: 4 job orders = 13.75 calls per job order

Visits to job orders = Average number of visits made to get each job order e.g. 3 visits: 4 job orders = 0.75 visits to 1 job order.

The example gives us average hours worked per temp of 29.86 – let's call it 30. If your weekly target is to increase your hours by 100 hours, then you can calculate that you need 3.33 job orders per week in addition to those you already have. From your recorded statistics, you will need to make at least 45.78 (13.73 x 3.33) or 46 calls to get the 3.33 job orders.

46 calls: 5 days = 9.2 calls per day every day. If you don't make this number of calls, you're *not* going to get the 100 hours you need that week. The only way to be able to decrease the amount of calls you need to make is to get better at making them, i.e. improve your call to job order ratio, which can be done through training and practice.

PART TWO

FOR MANAGERS AND RECRUITMENT BUSINESS OWNERS

Up till now I've covered the micro detail of how to set up and work on a temp desk from a consultant's viewpoint. In this part of the book I want to provide a macro view from a recruitment business owner's point of view. These chapters address what you need to think about in setting up your business, how you grow the business through monitoring and developing your staff's efficiencies, the finance structures you need, and understanding what factors impact on the future value of a recruitment agency – just in case you have visions of selling up for a massive profit and sailing into the sunset!

Sometimes consultants start their own recruitment businesses, but without a macro view, they can end up merely creating a job for themselves rather than a viable business.

As always I believe that you need to get experts in to cover the areas where you lack expertise yourself. So for this part of the book, I've chosen three experts in their own fields to share their perspectives about what's important.

CHAPTER 16

INTERVIEW WITH NIGEL HARSE

DIRECTOR OF THE RECRUITMENT INDUSTRY BENCHMARKING (RIB) REPORT

Nigel Harse was my old boss at Ecco in the 1990s and undoubtedly my success in this industry has partly been due to standing on his shoulders. He taught me how to look for markets even when there didn't seem to be any, to respect the full process he described, and to measure, measure, measure – as what you measure, you can improve!

Nigel was hugely successful in growing a national recruitment company in a climate when all our competitors were contracting, closing branches and selling off brands under their umbrellas. Nigel's particular skill was his ability to galvanise a team (even during an economic recession) to believe in ourselves and the 'process'. Nigel broke the recruitment process down and measured everyone's input and output, which is what enabled him to grow both his staff and the business. I know from many current recruitment business owners that they dislike the idea of keeping statistics and the culture they believe it brings. But you will see from my interview with Nigel Harse that it depends on how you use the statistics you collect. Are you using them to look for parts of the process that need improving? Or are you using them to clobber your staff over the head?

More about Nigel and the full service he provides can be found in the biographies at the end of this book.

Nigel graciously agreed to be interviewed by me for this chapter. Nigel's input is interesting for a couple of reasons. Firstly, the RIB Report he created collates data from 113 recruitment companies across all sectors in Australia and New Zealand on a monthly basis and has done so for the last ten years. This means that Nigel has up-to-the-minute information on what the top performers are billing as well as the average billers and the low performers. This data is essential if you want to know how you stack up against your peers in the industry. While the names of the companies are kept confidential, participants still get a complete picture of what is possible out there. Nigel goes on to say, 'It may be that you *are* a high performer, but you didn't realise it. Or maybe you think you're a top biller, but find that you're actually pretty average compared to what others are billing in the marketplace. There is no point in kidding yourself about your results, if you know what the best are achieving, then you know what to aim for'. As a professional, it's important that you don't work in isolation and that you are really aware of where you stand and importantly what you need to do to improve. Imagine if elite athletes operated in a vacuum and refused to measure their performance. They simply wouldn't know the level of performance needed to make the grade, or whether their training was improving their performance or not.

Secondly, Nigel came to Australia from the UK to establish and build Ecco Personnel and was my boss from 1990 to1995 (Ecco merged with Adia in 1996). This was during the recession, the one we 'had to have' in Australia when interest rates peaked at 17.5% and the unemployment rate was close to 11%. Yet during this time he managed to steer his team, of which I was a very happy member, to growth and profit in a market where many jobs had disappeared. I wanted his view on what has changed in the temporary recruitment industry.

Unsurprisingly, Nigel is a big fan of measuring activities because he believes it's important to *know* that you are honouring your commitments and doing what you promised your clients. If you don't measure things how do you find the areas you need to improve? He makes a clear and eloquent point about the difference between being 'in control' and 'controlling'.

Being in control is about doing the right activities and measuring them, so you can improve your efficiencies. If you don't know what you're doing, it's like working in the dark. Nigel also believes that as a manager, you have a *duty* to grow your people. It's your responsibility to make it clear to them that their challenge in taking on the role is to demonstrate that they are as good as yourself or even better. If you don't measure activities, then you either don't care or you're shirking from your responsibilities. 'Controlling' is when you measure the activities but then don't use the numbers for anything other than beating people over the head with.

Back when Nigel started in recruitment in 1977, he had to report on 20 different numbers every day, which included:

- tomorrow starters
- starters later in the week
- how many temps didn't show up at their assignment
- how many jobs taken that day
- how many advance orders were taken
- how many current assignments were extended
- how many jobs were filled
- how many jobs were unfilled and lost
- how many new temps were starting work
- how many candidates were interviewed
- how many temps were currently working
- how many reference checks were conducted
- average value of time sheet
- average hours worked by each temp
- average margin as a percentage of pay *or* as a markup of pay *or* as gross profit per hour, which are three ways to look at the same figure

Essentially it is all about measuring your *process*, so you can work on the parts that need strengthening. Once you have mastered the basic process and fine-tuned it, you can then progress to a higher level of problem solving. An example Nigel shared from blue-collar recruitment was when he approached a large tyre-manufacturing company who had experienced ongoing problems meeting their targets on a particular production line. Nigel asked them to give him full autonomy in running the production line with the people he saw fit. He staffed the line with temporaries – lots of mums who worked on a part-time afternoon and evening basis. Within one month they reached the full production quota for the first time. 'This was all about using our skill and knowledge to solve a problem, thus adding real bottom-line benefit and value to the client's business. Sadly, this is a far cry from the approach of many order takers out there who call themselves temp "consultants".'

Nigel points out that there is a *big* difference between the 'order takers' and the good temp consultants who are 'order *makers*'. Order makers sell people, their skills and concepts, and they make suggestions, which in essence is true consulting.

Here is Nigel's advice for people starting or working on a temp desk:

- Sell what you've got first, i.e. sell the temps you already have, the ones that are available or will be available, otherwise you could be making lots of calls and end up with jobs you can't fill.
- You have to have an inherent desire to keep a growing temp or contractor workforce working. You have to commit to finding ongoing jobs for them. In other words, it's *not* good enough that you only call them *if* you have something. First and foremost it is your job to find them ongoing work; you should understand that they are relying on you to keep them busy so they can pay their bills. If you do keep them busy they will reward you with trust, flexibility and loyalty, which can pay great dividends.
- You have to be prepared to deal with and solve problems that arise from managing people. Problems will arise, and your chance to shine will be through taking prompt affirmative action – you need to grab the bull by the horns! We are problem solvers.

- You must have a willingness to keep control and stay on top of the process of placing the right people quickly, checking they have settled in, ensuring that all time sheets are processed through the payroll and that people are paid correctly and on time, every time.
- A good temp consultant is someone who can juggle and manage priorities – you have to be able to keep many balls in the air at a time, and there is always much to be done! Do the important things constantly because being successful needs a consistent and balanced approach.
- If you have been gathering and keeping up to date with relevant market intelligence on your competitor agencies, who they work with and what they provide, it's much easier to find jobs for your temps. You will have a list of your competitors' clients to speak to. You could have a temp who has previously worked with that company through another provider and be able to offer that temp back to the client What better way to break the ice!
- To be a successful temp consultant you have to be committed to spending as much time on the phone finding jobs as you do interviewing and finding temps (compared to perm consultants, who spend most of their time finding people).

When I asked Nigel how temp recruitment has changed since the 1990s, he said we have lost an opportunity to build face-to-face relationships with temps and clients by offering them online time sheets and online invoicing. Gone are the days when temps had to either bring in their time sheets or pick up their pay cheques, which meant you got to see or speak with your temps once a week. He says that the 'essence of belonging' for temps is critical; without it we have little loyalty from the temps as they don't feel that we care in the same way. In today's environment we must engineer other ways to build a bond between the temps and the agency. When asked what ideas he might have, Nigel said: 'Perhaps a monthly get-together, which could be in different forms. Maybe you provide them with training, or it may be something social.' He considers this aspect of building and cementing a bond so critical that he would even consider paying them to come in for an hour, so the temps don't feel like they're doing it just for the agency. After all it's a partnership, where the temps agree to work for and be loyal to an agency and the agency commits to and provides continuous work for the temps.

CHAPTER 17

HOW TO OBTAIN FUNDING FOR A TEMP BUSINESS

DAVID PAYNE
DIRECTOR OF BOOK BUILDERS

In this chapter David Payne gives us a valuable insight into the different options for funding a business, and more importantly, doing it without jeopardising your family home or other personal assets. David outlines what you need to think about if you want to secure funding to grow a temp desk. This is helpful as it's hard to ask relevant questions when you don't know what you don't know. This chapter will give an insight into what questions you need to ask a potential lender and also what they might want to ask you.

I first met David when he attended my temp desk master class workshop in Perth a few years back. Two things impressed me about David: he was there to learn about the consulting side of recruitment, so he could add value to his recruitment clients even though he is a CFO and not directly involved with the day-to-day running of a temp desk; and he is a finance guy who can and does speak layman's language. I don't know about you, but I find there are few accountants who actually speak in a way that makes ordinary people interested in hearing about finance. David and I have kept in touch since that time and I was delighted when he offered to write the chapter on funding.

Enjoy his insights, and to read more about David and the service he provides, see the biographies at the back of the book.

GETTING STARTED

Have you thought about starting a temp business, but asked yourself, 'How on earth would I get the funding to do this?'

Or perhaps you're already in business but you're wondering if you've got the best deal on your finance. Or worse, saying 'I can't take on more contractors as I don't have the working capital'.

If you get the funding and business discipline correct from day one, there is no reason why you cannot achieve what another of my clients has done, which is to start and sell in less than five years a temp business with turnover of more than $13 million per annum on start-up capital of $15,000.

THE SKY IS THE LIMIT – WHY GETTING THE FUNDING RIGHT IS SO CRITICAL TO YOUR LONG-TERM SUCCESS

No matter whether you're thinking of starting a temp business, or you want to grow your existing business, you need to work out how much working capital is required, and what type of funding suits your requirements.

It is important that you invest the time to get your funding right, as to get it wrong may result in business failure and potentially losing your personal assets (such as your family home).

Depending on your clients and the mix of your receivables ledger at any point in time, debtor-finance funders will typically lend up to 90% of an invoice, including the GST amount (in rare cases a funder may fund up to 85% of the invoice value against blue chip customers). The good news for you is that, depending on your margin, 80% of your invoice may in fact cover 100% of the cost of your temps and contractors. This is demonstrated below. I have used contractors as the example, using a day rate, rather than temps who are paid by the hour. The principle is the same.

Employee Cost (including on-costs)	$880
Markup at 30%	$264
Charge Rate (excluding GST)	$1,144
Charge Rate (including GST)	$1,258
Funding at 80% Charge Rate (including GST)	$1,006

Therefore, with the right funding in place and depending on the markup, you may be able to pay an unlimited number of temporaries. That being said, you cannot look at your markup percentage in isolation from the overhead costs of running temps and contractors.

HOW MUCH FUNDING?

You have just seen how you can fund unlimited growth of your temp pool, but you know that cash is king and news travels fast, and you are probably worried that if you run out of cash to pay wages, your reputation will be ruined. That is why it is critical that you calculate your cash requirements to ensure that you have a facility in place sufficient to meet them. Before approaching your accountant for assistance in calculating your requirements, you need to consider the following:

- How many temps or contractors will you employ? This will help determine the facility limit and thus whether you use a bank or an alternative lender.
- Establishing your margins. This can be tricky because competitors will be unlikely to tell you their numbers, so you really need to do the market research. Prior industry experience, finding a mentor and/or talking to someone with extensive industry experience are useful ways to gather such knowledge. Take into account that as funders generally only fund up to 80% of the invoice value, any difference must be covered by the business owners, so a higher margin will mean finding less funding from personal sources.

- Your niche – as a rule of thumb, the more you specialise, the higher the margin you can charge.
- Expense control – avoid spending money too early on things you can manage without. It is always concerning when owners of new businesses start spending the cash provided by the funders on fancy cars and flash offices when that money may be required to fund essential overhead costs.
- Security – if you secure your funding against your home, for example, what happens when the business continues to grow and you run out of equity?
- Once you have considered the above, it is time to work out your funding requirements with the help of your accountant.

Example

Try to find a potential client who will support you in your new venture by paying your invoices within seven days. Short payment terms will improve your cash flow, reduce your risk and make it easier to start your temp recruitment business.

(The below example is based on contractors who are paid a day rate, which differs from temporaries, who are paid an hourly rate.)

Imagine having 20 contractors with a client who supports your business by paying your invoices in seven to 14 days. At a day rate of $800+GST and a margin of 10%, you would have to find funding of $55,000, for a return of $105,000 after three months. Not a bad return on your investment for what might only require you to take out an overdraft on your home.

It is unlikely that you will find more than one client to support your new business with favourable payment terms, and as the funding requirements increase with increased payment terms, you need to consider how to build your business beyond one client.

Let's say for example that you have the one fast paying client mentioned above and a second client who pays on terms of 30 days from end of month, each with 20 contractors at a day rate of $800+GST and a margin of 10%. In this case, you would have to find funding of $209,000, for a gross contribution of $209,000 after three months. Not so attractive any more – also, you will have to consider when the equity in your home will no longer be enough to fund the business.

As you can see, as soon as your new business has to start trading on normal terms, more funding is required.

If you are not lucky enough to find one client to support your new business and pay your invoices within seven to 14 days, the numbers really start to look scary. With 20 contractors at a day rate of $800+GST and a margin of 10%, you would have to find funding of $370,000, for a gross contribution of $104,000 after three months – no longer sounds so enticing to set up your own business, does it?

However, it can be easy if you get the funding right from day one, supported by the right systems and people. You should be able to grow your business without the stress of worrying about cash flow.

HOW TO ASK A LENDER FOR FUNDING

Now that you have calculated the amount of funding required, the next stage is to construct a proposal detailing funding requirements for your potential lenders.

The facility limit that you require will determine how much work you need to do before approaching the lender. If the required debt facility is less than $1.5 million, you may be able to avoid having to provide detailed forecasts by working with a good account manager who can help you through the process. If the debt facility is more than $1.5 million, be prepared to pay an accountant to prepare a 'three-way forecast' (profit and loss, balance sheet and cash flows).

If you require a facility in excess of $1.5 million, make sure that you get the right help. Identifying your funding requirements can be expensive – expect to pay $20,000 to $30,000 for an expert to help you through the process, including calculating your cash requirements, preparing detailed three-way forecasts and liaising with the funder. Not all accountants are trained in or know how to prepare a forecast to support a $1.5 million-plus debtor-finance facility – don't take it for granted that your tax agent will be able to do this work for you as it is a specialised area of accounting. If your accountant does not know what a three-way forecast is or understand how to incorporate a finance facility into a forecast model, let them keep preparing your tax but don't burn money getting them to help obtain your funding – it could do more harm than good and cost you a lot of money at the same time.

It is important that you look at your funding request as if you were the lender. Consider what they would need to know in order to grant you funding approval. That means you need to:

- Be completely professional in your approach.
- Leverage off professionals you already know to connect you with sympathetic lenders. If you are approaching a major bank, don't just go to your local branch – they may be hamstrung by restrictive lending criteria. If possible, go as high up in the bank as you can, for example the state lending manager, as he or she may be able to negotiate better terms and rates than a local business banker. You can use LinkedIn to identify these professionals.
- If possible, take your accountant with you – especially if they already have a relationship with the head of invoice finance for a particular bank. This won't convey any shortcomings on your part. Rather it will show that you know how to leverage expertise and will instil confidence in the lender.
- Try to avoid taking along an accountant who does not understand the forecast model, the type of funding required or how you're going manage the facility.
- Prepare for any of the lenders' concerns, anticipate their questions and formulate contingency answers before the preliminary meeting. Your accountant can help with this. Remember that the bigger the risk you are asking them to take, the more they are exposing themselves to potential fraud or business failure. The higher the risk, the higher the interest.
- Compare the offers of various lenders. Never just take the first offer you

receive, and remember that 'everything is negotiable', no matter what they tell you about bank policy.

- Build a relationship with the financier. Make friends with the banker. They are human too and are more inclined to be more helpful if they know you, like you and learn to trust you.

Remember that if you do all of the above you can always go back to the lender and renegotiate as the situation changes, but in order to set yourself up to succeed, you ideally need to have the loan structured in a flexible way. That's why debtor finance (factoring) may be more advantageous than equity finance (where investors contribute finance in return for a share in the business). Equity is limited to the amount of capital that you or other shareholders have available – plus with debtor finance the bank is not going to ask for half of your profit when you eventually sell the business.

IS IT TIME TO RENEGOTIATE?

Are your current funding arrangements holding you back from growing your temp recruitment business? Does your funder impose a lot of conditions on the funding that they provide you, such as dollar sub-limits per customer or percentage limits? Is your funder reluctant to increase your limits? Do you think that you are paying too much in fees? Then it might be time to have a frank discussion with your funder about your business needs.

Before approaching your funder, you should be aware of the current market rates that you should be paying for funding. This can be achieved by speaking to your accountant to see if they have other clients with similar funding arrangements in place, or approaching other funding providers and asking for a quote.

When you are seeking market rates, it helps to understand the different service offerings the banks and non-banks provide and the terminology that they use. Many non-bank lenders have what they tend to call a 'service' fee, which includes the value-added services of debt collection or payroll processing; whereas banks have a 'facility' or 'line' fee, which does not include these services. The service fees charged by non-banks are calculated on a set percentage of the client invoice or payroll and can be in the range of 2% to 4%. As banks will not collect your outstanding invoices or process your payroll, their facility fee is lower than this. Therefore to compare apples with apples you need to work out how much it will cost you to outsource your collections or payroll to another provider, from which you can deduce what the non-bank is charging you compared to what you would be charged by a bank.

Depending on who your funder is, the service, line or facility fee will exclude the charge for what the banks call 'interest' and what the non-bank lenders call a 'discount charge'.

Once you have the current market rates for funding the type of facility that your business needs, you have the information to negotiate a better deal. You should always approach your existing funder, explain to them the constraints that the current funding facility is placing on your business growth and ask them to review your terms. It also doesn't hurt to let them know, in a nice way, that you have received rates from other funders – you don't have to tell them what the rates are.

THE KEY POINTS TO GET RIGHT

Once you have funding in place you need to manage it responsibly as you can easily get into financial trouble. To ensure that you are managing your money, the funder will require you to provide them with regular financial reports. In addition, from time to time the funder will come and visit you to complete an audit. Accordingly, it is vital that you do the following things:

- Make sure you get the timing of paying wages and invoicing customers right. That can make or break you. You should be paying your temps and contractors 2 to 3 days after you have raised the invoice to the client. (For PAYG temps you may be limited to paying them one day after you raise the invoice to the client due to award conditions, whereas for Pty Ltd contractors, payment terms are by negotiation – just the same way payment of your invoice is by negotiation.)
- Check and double-check your cash-flow forecast. It's the lifeblood of any business.

- Negotiate (or renegotiate) the right type of funding to suit your planned growth. If you do use equity funding, keep a really close eye on how near you are to the limits.
- Have in place, and be ready to explain to the funder, excellent systems to manage your payroll, invoicing, collections and purchase orders. Purchase-order management is required as your clients may not tell you that you have exceeded the limit of a purchase order, and if you don't have a system in place to alert you, you will not find out that a new purchase order is required until the invoice is overdue.
- Build a good support team around you – not just your staff. I'm talking about your accountant (a good management accountant, not just a tax accountant) and your banker (or other lender).

WHAT NOT TO DO

You have just successfully negotiated a facility – be it invoice finance, invoice factoring, or another type of facility that is based on the invoices that you raised. All of a sudden that debtors book of $200,000 has been taken by the funder and you have $160,000 in the bank. It looks like a lot, and thinking that you have cash to spare and not understanding the funding that you have in place can lead you into a false sense of security.

The owner of an eight-month-old temp business that had grown to have a turnover of $3 million per annum (annualised) had set up a finance facility based on factoring invoices. The owner was happy as he had plenty of cash and *thought* he was able to afford a new Range Rover. However, warning bells should have been going off, as in the first 12 to 18 months of a new business, no income tax, and possibly no GST, will have yet been paid. The owner was using a bookkeeper to maintain the accounts and was not tracking the liabilities properly; had spent the cash that the factoring company had put in the bank account, which should have been put aside for tax; and did not even realise that he should have been paying payroll tax. As he was relying on his bookkeeper to do the job of a qualified accountant he had not set up his accounting systems properly and did not know his true financial position. The result was that he could only manage his business by the cash balance in the bank account, and as the funder had 'filled up' the account the owner thought that he could start taking profits from the company before he should have.

Unfortunately, the aforementioned situation is not uncommon. There are many business owners signing up for finance without having the correct systems and processes in place to ensure that they can manage their obligations. Anyone considering taking on finance to fund a temp recruitment business needs to ensure that either they have the skill to manage the facility or that they hire someone who does.

As I said at the beginning, if you get everything right with your business there is no reason why you too cannot have a business with a $13 million-plus turnover on a $15,000 upfront investment – and with the right funding and business discipline in place the funder will take care of the rest so that you don't have to invest another dollar.

CHAPTER 18

HOW BUILDING A TEMP AND CONTRACT DESK IMPACTS BUSINESS EVALUATION

ROD HORE
DIRECTOR OF HHMC

In this chapter Rod Hore gives us a valuable insight into what buyers of recruitment businesses look for, which factors increase the value of the business and which factors don't, even though you might think they should! This chapter is largely extracted from an article previously published on the HHMC website.

Rod, whom I know through Nigel Harse, is well connected not just in the Australian market but on a global scale. He can speak knowledgeably about market trends anywhere in the world. Rod is a true professional who has great listening and follow-through skills – both important business skills that I'm constantly surprised (or should I say disappointed) that more people don't display. He is generous with his knowledge and if you're thinking of buying or selling a recruitment business, he is who you want to have on your team. Rod's full bio is in the biography section at the back of this book. In the meantime, enjoy his sage advice!

INTRODUCTION TO RECRUITMENT INDUSTRY BUSINESS VALUATIONS

Large businesses, such as those with an independent board, continually make strategy decisions to protect their sustainability. They will have strategies in place for finance, management, sales, clients, geographic coverage, product mix, and operations capability – in fact all aspects of business. An area of great focus is building sustainability into the businesses' revenue and profit forecasts. The board and executive are asking: what decisions should the business be taking to protect its future?

The adopted strategies will often forfeit high-return/high-risk options for 'steady' options that will deliver predictable revenue and profit. A business that can predict future revenue and profit will be less subject to catastrophic failure and thus will be valued more highly.

The same philosophy applies within the recruitment industry. It means that if you have a business with a substantial contribution from temp and contract services (a steady option), you will have a business with greater sustainability and higher value than a similar-sized business with little revenue from temp and contract services.

This chapter looks at some of the characteristics of business valuation in the recruitment industry and the impact temp and contract revenue has on this business valuation. There is a lot of misunderstanding about business valuations in general, but especially in the value of small-to-medium recruitment agencies.

It does need to be noted that there is very little published information on recruitment-agency valuations that is applicable to small-to-medium agencies. Press releases about large deals, especially if they involve listed companies, are misleading. Articles about deals in other countries can be misleading if applied to your market. Most of what happens in business deals with smaller companies in the recruitment industry is not published as it involves deals between private companies that are kept confidential.

WHAT WILL A BUYER PAY FOR?

There are many passionate agency owners that are justifiably proud of their achievements in market positioning, technology implementation, business processes, candidate databases and social media presence. Some are also proud of their logo, web page and even office location and fit-out.

These aspects of a business may add to the desirability of an agency, meaning more potential buyers may be interested in evaluating the business. But what a buyer will pay for a business will primarily be determined by the justified profit forecast for the immediate future.

Investment decisions by business owners needs to reflect this reality – all investment decisions should be about growing profit in a sustainable manner.

It should also be noted that longevity is rewarded. A business that has shown the ability to prosper through changes in business conditions and industry evolution will be rewarded with a lower risk rating when their business is being assessed. Conversely, start-up businesses (say less than three years) or a business that has not shown the ability to grow and adapt will be assessed accordingly.

WHY SUSTAINABILITY MATTERS

Looking at the past two or three years' financial performance is an important part of understanding a recruitment business's capability and potential. But this past performance is not an appropriate guide to future performance and hence not an appropriate guide to the business value.

For a services industry like recruitment, the business value may be thought of as the level of risk associated with a new owner generating profits in the future. The seller is asking the buyer to pay a multiple of future profits for the business. What generated profits in the past? Are those characteristics available for the new owner in the future? Aspects like client contracts, business development capability, key staff and market conditions all need to be evaluated by the potential buyer.

For these reasons, calculating the average of the past three years profit is not a relevant valuation method and is usually misleading.

The most important determinate of future revenue and profit is actually the size and quality of the temp and contract part of the business.

Any agency that is dominated by perm recruitment, no matter what its size or sector, will struggle to attract buyers and struggle to achieve a strong value for its business when compared to agencies that have a strong temp and contract focus.

A great example of this is executive search recruitment businesses. These businesses can be strongly branded, influential, profitable, even fast growing and large, but their sustainability is usually tied up with the performance of the senior search consultants. These senior resources own the client relationships, generate the job opportunities, and are instrumental in the execution of the recruitment process. If they want to exit the business, the value of the business exits as well. The sustainability of an executive search business and its value will be lower than other businesses.

HHMC talks about sustainability a lot. We like the definitions provided by Michael E Gerber in his classic book *The E-Myth: Why Most Businesses Don't Work and What to Do About It* (Ballinger Publishing Company, 1985), which taught us the difference between creating a job and building a business. Many small-business owners work *in* the business and are unable to lift themselves up to work *on* the business. They have created a job for themselves, often with restrictions on their earning capacity and work-life balance.

Smaller companies, almost by definition, struggle with sustainability – they may have single points of failure such as being reliant on one person for the majority of business development, or one person for the majority of billings, or one client for the majority of revenue. Any business that fails the sustainability test will not attract a standard valuation.

One of the very few ways an agency of less than, say, five consultants can attempt to prove sustainability is to run a strong temp and contract book.

HOW MUCH TEMP AND CONTRACT IS ENOUGH?

Not all countries have employment laws that encourage a contingent workforce. For example in Asia Pacific, staffing industry analysts quote New Zealand's staffing industry size as larger than other developed countries in the region such as Singapore and Hong Kong, and this is because of New Zealand's large contingent workforce. Even within countries, not all sectors sustain the same level of temp and contract recruitment – some specialist sectors are dominated by perm recruitment.

As a business strategy, you need to decide if you want your business to be held hostage to fluctuations in economic conditions that can have a dramatic negative effect on perm recruitment opportunities. If you are seeking to build a sustainable recruitment business then you need a strong contribution from temp and contract services.

If your business specialises in a sector that does not allow you to get at least 25% of gross profit contribution from temp and contract services, then a short-to-medium-term strategy should be to commence a complementary business that allows this contribution to grow. Yes, it is that important to the long-term sustainability and viability of your business.

For most small-to-medium recruitment businesses, we recommend the contribution to gross profit from temp and contract be 50% or greater.

Some recruitment sectors, such as IT, are dominated by temp and contract services. In these sectors, the contribution to gross profit should be above 50% and preferably 70%.

The larger the business, the greater these targets become. For example, a review of the financials of the largest global recruitment businesses shows that they achieve contribution from temp and contract above 90% – that is what is required to build predictability into businesses of that size.

There are exceptions. There are a few global recruitment companies that have built strong sales 'machines' that can compete and win perm assignments and have been able to do this successfully across geographies and through varied economic cycles. Similarly, there are a few executive search companies that have built strong, enduring global businesses. But they *are* the exception.

Not convinced?

We tend to have short memories when learning the lessons of history. The recent global financial crisis provided a number of sobering examples of recruitment agencies that had catastrophic failures when their perm-dominated businesses suffered revenue collapse. And these businesses were not all 'average' companies – some were award-winning leaders in their sector.

Other considerations

Building a temp and contract business comes with personal and business obligations that go far beyond those of a perm-only recruiter.

- Your business needs funding, either from retained cash reserves or from a debt facility. Every time you place a temp or contract person your business will use cash and you need the capability and capacity to manage that.
- Your business will need to be operationally sound, especially in the complex area of time sheets and payroll. Falter just once with payroll and your business reputation will be damaged.
- There will be a whole range of compliance obligations that relate to your business because of the employment relationship you have with the temps and contractors, and because you are managing other people's money.

A SUMMARY OF BUSINESS VALUATION

Some definitions

When discussing business sale results it is important to have a precise definition. Is it a share sale or an asset sale? Is working capital included or not? Are we discussing a multiple of profit before tax or a multiple of profit after tax?

The most common structure used for the purchase of small-to-medium recruitment agencies is the purchase of business assets for cash.

For consistency, unless otherwise qualified, we will here discuss small-to-medium recruitment agency value as a multiple of normalised profit before tax excluding working capital.

'Normalised profit' means making adjustments to the revenue and expenses to reflect the business as if someone else was running it. The major adjustments are usually related to shareholders' expenses (some private expenses may be able to be removed) and adjustments to shareholders' salary packages (they may be paying themselves more or less than market rates).

'Net working capital', for this purpose, is most easily described as cash plus debtors less creditors less staff entitlements (such as annual leave).

Deal structure affects business value

Purchasers are looking to reduce the risk to generating future profits. Sellers are looking to exit their business with as few risks or time delays as possible. The balance of these two requirements impacts the value of a business, and is a unique negotiation for each buyer and seller situation.

At one extreme, if a seller wants to sell a business for 100% cash up front and leave the business immediately they will receive less for the business, because of the high risk to the purchaser.

However by assisting the purchaser through participating in the business for a period following the sale and reducing the buyer's risk by accepting part payment up front and the balance on future performance, they can maximise the amount the purchaser will be prepared to pay.

If a recruitment agency displays strong corporate characteristics then it may attract the attention of professional investors such as private equity companies or larger agencies. These corporate characteristics usually include: little influence from the founders, multiple shareholders, a strong management team, an independent board, a healthy balance sheet, strong financial facilities, strong geographic and/or sector coverage, revenue sustainability, a strong client mix, and significant size. However owner/operator businesses don't tend to have these characteristics.

For owner/operator companies there is no such thing a standard deal, but with reference to all the above comments, the valuation of small-to-medium recruitment agencies is usually considered along these lines:

- Deal structure usually involves about half being paid up front and the remainder paid on the future performance of the business over an earn-out period of between six and 24 months.

- The multiple of normalised profit before tax most often falls in the range of 2.5 to 4.0. This has not changed for over 15 years but profitability has certainly varied over this period.
- Those small-to-medium agencies that are sustainable are mostly valued in the 2.5 to 3.0 multiple range. A number of positive characteristics will be required to justify a multiple over 3.0.
- However many small-to-medium agencies (maybe as many as 50% of all agencies) fail the sustainability test and are valued at less than a multiple of 2.5.
- Many agencies fall into the 'personal services' category and are not able to have a business valuation applied at all. In these circumstances the value of work in progress or the value of the temp book may be the value of the business, or an arrangement can be made to transition employment arrangements to a new company.

ADVICE FOR SMALL-TO-MEDIUM AGENCY OWNERS

There is no single correct strategy for a recruitment agency owner in terms of growth, size, sector, or business mix. But you need to understand the implications of your chosen strategy. Don't drift into a particular business mix; make a conscious decision. For example, if you want to run a small, specialist, perm-dominated business that generates good cash returns, then that is a valid strategy, *but* the equity value of the business will be low and the risk of business failure will increase.

All agency owners should have a wealth creation strategy that is more regular, consistent and sustainable than 'one day sell my business for a lot of money'. Research discussed in *The Millionaire Mind* by Thomas J Stanley (Andrews McMeel Publishing, 2000), suggests that consistently seeking to reward shareholders, in balance with continued business investment, is the most successful wealth creation strategy for small-to-medium business owners.

Certainly one road to equity value is to build a temp desk and make it a meaningful part of your business. You will sleep better and you will create greater wealth.

CHAPTER 19

TEMP DESK IMPLEMENTATION CHECKLIST

In this chapter I've provided a checklist of things you need to establish in order to implement a temp desk within your business. If you already have a temp desk, you can see what else you may need. If you're starting a temp desk from scratch, you can use the checklist to ensure you don't miss anything.

SETTING UP THE TEMP DESK

- Create a list of job categories in your niche.
- Become familiar with the applicable awards.
- Calculate market hourly rates: determine permanent market salaries and divide by 52 weeks and then by 38 hours (including 25% casual loading); and determine on-costs.
- Determine your positioning in market and margins with regard to what competitors pay and charge.
- Hire consultants with a growth mindset.
- Ensure on-going quality training of consultants.

BUILDING A TEMP BASE

Ensure you have in place:

- A variety of sources of temps: advertising, referrals, payrollers (i.e. temps you are payrolling for a client), current people from perm database
- Forms to be filled out when consultants take a job order
- Interview forms with the relevant interview questions for temp applicants (incorporated into your permanent interview form or a separate form)
- Written temp agreement stating terms and including permission for you to contact referees supplied
- Written client contract stating terms of business, hourly rates and temp-to-perm fees
- An established set of 'rules' for temps and clients
- Relevant testing
- A checklist of required tickets, e.g. forklift licence, white card for the construction industry
- A checklist of work permits and visas, e.g. permanent resident or student visa
- Reference check forms (questions are slightly different for temps than for perm candidates)
- Bank account details form and superannuation form
- Time sheets, online or physical
- Induction process for WHS (work health and safety)
- Temp info database
- Availability list

BACK OFFICE REQUIREMENTS

- Payroll

- Invoicing
- Compliance i.e. superannuation, payroll tax, work cover
- Cash flow
- Financing/factoring

HIGHER LEVEL DECISIONS

Questions to consider:

- Temp guarantee: what will it be?
- Market and niche, e.g. government or health industry? Where do you pitch your service? Who are the main competitors in your niche? What are they offering?
- Organisational structure: e.g. territorial, vertical markets, specialisations
- Staff rewards and incentives
- Testing: how conducted, online or in office? On what type of package, e.g. Skillcheck, Qwiz?

AFTERWORD

When I think back to the very first recruitment company I worked for (which I don't usually mention as the company wasn't very ethical and therefore it was a very short-lived experience), where they gave me the classifieds section of the *Sydney Morning Herald* and asked me to call all the job advertisers to see if they would agree to let me recruit for them, and the *White Pages* I was given at my second job where I was asked to make 30 cold calls a day, I am thankful that the industry has progressed from those dark days. In some ways it's a miracle that the recruitment industry was able to survive those times as unsurprisingly the wider business community had a bad impression of us when practices like those were going on.

Now many recruitment companies know the value of training their consultants and are willing to invest both time and money to ensure that their consultants have a solid skill base and can portray our industry in a professional light. While I applaud the companies who show foresight and courage, I occasionally come across companies who are still unwilling to take the leap to really invest in their people. They seem to be more of the glass-half-empty persuasion, thinking 'what if I invest in training this person and then they leave me?' or 'what if they aren't the right one, then I've wasted my money?'

I noted in *BRW*'s '50 Best Places to Work in 2013' that there were 3 recruitment companies on the list. Two of them I've had the privilege and pleasure of working with as coaching clients and the third made enquiries at one point. I am not saying they were on that list because of my training, but rather perhaps they were on that list because they sought training for their staff. The two companies in question are always on the quest to make their consultants better at their jobs, so they can better serve their clients. And by doing this, they create happy, loyal employees who stay, deliver good service and produce results. In business as in life, we need to be driven by courage to do what we know works rather than by fear of failure. As we say in coaching, there is no such thing as failure, only feedback. When we look at everything as feedback, that's when we grow both personally and professionally.

My desire to write this 'how-to' book was driven by wanting to make it easier and more profitable for consultants and recruitment business owners working in the industry. Through trial and error, training, study, experience and self evaluation I have learnt many lessons that I've been able to pass on. As I mentioned in some of the examples in the book, some lessons took me many months to learn as I was figuring them out as I went along.

So what *are* the secrets to running a lucrative temp desk?

- Have a growth mindset; be willing to learn from any experience.
- Don't label yourself as it limits your potential, which is truly limitless.
- Be open to learning new skills; then practice, practice, practice so you can reach mastery.
- Be disciplined enough to consistently follow the client and temp best practice process every time.

My wish is that you use the processes and tips in this book to catapult you to the success you deserve. All you need is a growth mindset and to be willing to practice, practice and practice your skills, so you can reach mastery. What is so gratifying is that in this industry, you actually get to make a real difference to people's lives and when you do it well, you also get to reap the monetary rewards.

Lastly, nothing ever happens in isolation, and I've had a few shoulders to stand on in bringing this book into the world. My thanks to the following:

Nicholas Beames – for writing the foreword

Nigel Harse – for his generosity in letting me interview him about his vast knowledge of vital metrics

Rod Hore – for his generosity in contributing the chapter on business evaluation

David Payne – for his generosity in contributing the chapter on getting funding

John Plummer – for his constructive feedback on the manuscript

Last but not least, Roz Hopkins my publishing director, who made this whole process easy and manageable for a rookie author.

If you want to contact any of the contributors in this book or myself to stand on our shoulders, please don't hesitate. It's the thirst to learn more that keeps you one step ahead of your competition. The industry is forever evolving and we need to evolve with it!

Please register on my website: www.youniquecoaching.com.au for more articles and resources about recruitment, business development and leadership tools.

Email me: sophie@youniquecoaching.com.au to engage in further conversations about temps or any other recruitment-related matters.

Wishing you every success,

Sophie

BIOGRAPHIES

SOPHIE ROBERTSON

Sophie Robertson was born to parents from Shanghai, and grew up in Hong Kong, Denmark, Canada and the United States before coming to Australia in 1985. Sophie went to school in Canada, the US and Denmark, where she also attended the University of Copenhagen. Sophie has lived on four continents and speaks English, Danish and Chinese (Shanghai dialect).

Since coming to Australia, Sophie has graduated from the Institute of Personnel Consultants, now part of the Recruitment and Consulting Services Association (RCSA). Sophie is a current member of RCSA and holds the designation of Fellow (FRCSA). Sophie has completed her Certificate IV in Life Coaching and is a member of the Australian and New Zealand Institute of Coaching (ANZI). Career-wise Sophie has spent 18 years in various positions with recruitment companies. Since 2007 Sophie has been training, coaching and mentoring recruiters and recruitment business owners.

A career highlight was when Sophie was promoted from rookie consultant to branch manager of a recruitment agency within 12 months, and went on to run the most profitable branch out of 30 branches nationally. Sophie later joined a boutique recruitment firm and held various roles including business development manager, general manager and business development director. During her recruitment career, Sophie secured many major accounts; some of which are mentioned in this book.

She has a special knack of analysing what a client really needs even when the clients are slow to articulate those needs. Sophie believes that communication often happens on two levels; the spoken level and the hidden message behind the words chosen. Sophie's personal motto is: 'It can't hurt to ask'. In other words better to ask and get a 'no' than not opening the door to the possibility of a resounding 'yes'.

Sophie was the resident expert on recruiterdaily.com.au from 2008 to 2011, where she contributed over 100 articles on recruitment matters. Her opinions on career coaching have been sought by publications as diverse as the *Sydney Morning Herald*, *Marie Claire* and *Body and Soul* magazine.

Sophie sits on the advisory panel of the recruitment company People for Purpose; whose vision is a thriving 'for-purpose' (non-profit) sector where organisations are able to access and develop outstanding leaders and executives, maximising their potential for social impact.

NIGEL HARSE – THE RIB REPORT

Nigel Harse is an experienced recruitment industry specialist, commentator and mentor who has a great passion for assisting firms that strive to achieve superior business results by helping them take the steps needed to go from average to great performance levels.

He commenced his recruitment career in 1977 as a consultant on an industrial temp desk with HMS Recruitment (Hestair plc) in the UK. In 13 years he gained six promotions and in 1989 was appointed regional director with profit responsibility for a diverse network of recruitment operations (industrial, office support, medical, hospitality) throughout the UK. He was approached by Ecco to join them and in late 1990 as the recession started, he moved to Australia to manage two underperforming acquisitions for Ecco, the world's second largest global staffing firm.

In five years, he took the company from $7 million to over $75 million in sales through an organically grown national network. He personally recruited and trained every staff member and expanded the operation from nine branches in two states to Australia-wide with 35 branches and more than 150 employees. Under his leadership, the Australian subsidiary was consistently ranked in the top three performing operations of the worldwide Ecco Group, and its reputation throughout the '90s for being one of the fastest growing Australian firms around was well founded.

During the same period Nigel was instrumental in the creation, development and delivery of training for the special interest groups within the NAPC (National Association of Personnel Consultants, now part of the RSCA). He served as a councillor for five years and is a former Victorian vice president of the NAPC.

After six years at the helm and achieving and exceeding every objective that had been agreed with Ecco, Nigel decided it was time to move on. Six months later Ecco became Adecco.

Nigel was by invitation appointed a director of the listed firm Catalyst in October 2001 until it was sold to Skilled in 2006; he was also CEO and partner of MDB & Co (accountants and business advisors) and as CEO he established and built MDB Insurance Solutions which he sold in 2008.

In 2003 in response to ongoing requests from industry owners who wanted to have some way of measuring their results and successes against their peers, he created the RIB (Recruitment Industry Benchmark) Report. In Australia it is the only extensive report on business performance specifically for recruitment agencies and it's now regarded as the nation's most reliable and well-respected measure of how the general recruitment industry is performing. See more at www.ribreport.com.au. For recruitment business owners and managers with a P&L responsibility, this report is essential reading. Nigel is offering a free sample of the RIB report to readers. To obtain this invaluable report, email deb@ribreport.com.au; code: Sophie.

Through his endeavours as a business coach and mentor to a number of recruitment firms throughout Australia and New Zealand, he's become a trusted advisor and proven specialist in recruitment industry business performance and operational benchmarking.

DAVID PAYNE – BOOK BUILDERS

David Payne brings a unique skill set to small-to-medium sized companies from his corporate experience as a CFO and during his eight years' experience with Ferrier Hodgson, Australia's largest corporate recovery accounting firm. As David worked in all facets of insolvency accounting and turned around businesses in financial distress, he saw that many businesses failed simply because they lacked proper accounting and financial functions and did not have the knowledge to manage their cash flow. David saw a gap in the market for providing this expertise to business owners so they could grow and prosper.

Thus, in 2006, David co-founded Book Builders with the goal of providing companies with outsourced solutions to manage their accounting, payroll and financial functions. Today, the company provides small-to-medium-sized businesses with the right tools and systems for accounting clarity and management of their businesses, enabling them not only to grow, but to also succeed in their mission and complete their exit strategies.

His service focuses on ensuring businesses are fully compliant with all financial reporting and wage documentation regulations. In addition he and his team of fully qualified professionals provide credit control services and can assist in accessing the best financial loan terms to grow any temp and contract business. Working with David means businesses have full access to CFO services but without the burden of having to hire a CFO full time.

David is a chartered accountant with over 20 years' accounting, finance and payroll experience including a number of years as the CFO of a large Australian health company, so David not only understands businesses, but he also knows that good financial management is a large part of what makes them successful.

Although David's systems and processes have been streamlined to adapt easily to different industries, over the last few years Book Builders have specialised and become experts in supporting on-hire businesses.

David has also developed long-standing relationships with many leading financial institutions which now benefits his clients as they can be assured of access to the best funding facilities.

See www.davidpayne.com.

ROD HORE – HHMC

In 1998 Rod Hore founded HHMC Australia to provide buying and selling advisory services to the recruitment industry.

He is responsible for the leadership of the group and for undertaking advisory roles and merger and acquisitions assignments.

Rod has a special interest in providing a range of advisory services and seminars assisting recruitment organisations to achieve their growth and sustainability objectives. He is an accomplished speaker on issues affecting business owners and a regular contributor to recruitment industry publications and the HHMC social media channels.

Rod has been involved in service industries since 1980, commencing his career in information technology. Prior to founding HHMC, Rod had a 20-year record of leadership with local and global information technology consulting companies, working throughout Australia.

Rod has a business degree in information processing and is a graduate of the Australian Institute of Company Directors (AICD). Through HHMC, Rod is an active supporter of the Asia Pacific recruitment industry. See www.hhmc.com.au.

GLOSSARY

Blue-collar – workers who do labouring, picking and packing, driving forklifts, etc.

Casual – a worker hired directly by a client company on a non-permanent basis. Sometimes blue- and orange-collar temps are referred to as 'casuals' although they are sourced and paid through an agency.

Contingent workforce – "contingent" refers to a non-permanent workforce or employee, whether their employment status is casual, temp or contractor.

Contractor – a person who works for a company under his or her own company name. Contractors pay their own workers' compensation, superannuation, public liability and professional indemnity insurances. They will have their own ABN (Australian Business Number). Contractors are usually paid by the day rather than by the hour. Hourly rates are governed by awards, while contractor conditions aren't, as they have higher day rates which negate the relevant award or their higher skill levels simply aren't covered by awards.

Orange-collar – people working in mining or mining-related construction work; the orange comes from the orange high visibility vests that are worn on site.

On-hire – the term used to describe a person who is recruited and paid by an agency and then 'hired on' to a client. This term defines the legal relationship between the agency, the on-hired person and the client company in Australia and New Zealand. Recruitment companies that offer temporary/contracting/casual staff are also referred to as on-hire recruitment companies.

On-hire company – a recruitment company that on-hires temporary staff to client companies; its role being the sourcing and screening of all on-hire staff while also taking care of compliance matters relating to the provision of an on-hire employee.

Labour hire – a general term used to describe the hiring of temps and casuals, usually unskilled blue collar workers.

Perm – short for permanent recruitment, e.g. a perm consultant is a recruiter who recruits permanent staff for clients rather than temps and contractors.

RCSA – Recruitment Services and Consulting Association, Australia and New Zealand; the recruitment industry's educational and governing body. Membership and adherence to the RCSA's Code of Ethics is entirely voluntary as the industry is still not regulated in Australia and New Zealand.

Staffing – in Australia this is used as a generic term to describe temp and perm placements whereas in the US, this term is used predominantly for temps.

Temp – short for a temporary worker paid by an agency to work for a client. Temps are traditionally used in office support roles, however this term can be used for anyone who works on a temporary, i.e. not permanent, basis.

Temp metrics – quantitative measurements used to track performance and to forecast the activity required to reach specified goals, such as increased number of temp hours or profitability or anything else.

White-collar – refers to most people working in an office, from office support to skilled staff e.g. drafts people. Note that more highly-skilled people such as those at middle and upper management levels prefer to be called contractors.

Printed in Great Britain
by Amazon

34504296R00102